$20

Toku Tini
(Self Deception)

"So motherfucker kiss the ground."
- Shane MacGowan

[handwritten signatures]

Also by Michael O'Leary

Poetry

Flipside to the Ballad of John and Yoko
Surrogate Children (with Sandra Bell/Brian Hare)
Ten Sonnets, Myths and Legends of Love
Undiscovered Voyage (with Litia F. Alaelua)
Livin' ina Aucklan' (with illustrations by John Pule)
Before and After
Shake Speer's Faith
Con Art: Selected Poems
Ka Atu I Koopua — Out of the Deep
He Waiatanui kia Aroha
T.A.B. Ula Rasa

Fiction

Straight
Out of It
The Irish Annals of New Zealand
Noa/Nothing I
Unlevel Crossings

As editor

Wrapper

Non-fiction

Gone West: Waikumete Cemetery
Grafton Cemetery

Literary Criticism

It's All in the Mind You Know
Alternative Small Press Publishing
in New Zealand

Toku Tinihanga
(Self Deception)

selected poems
1982-2002

Michael O'Leary

With a Foreword by
F. W. N. Wright

HEADWORX
WELLINGTON

Poems © Michael O'Leary, 2003
Foreword © F. W. N. Wright, 2003

First published 2003

ISBN 0-473-09006-6

Published by

HeadworX Publishers
26 Grant Rd, Thorndon
Wellington
Aotearoa / New Zealand
http://headworx.eyesis.co.nz

Printed by

Astra Print

HeadworX® is a registered
trademark of HeadworX Publishers

Typeset by HeadworX Publishers
in Veljovic Book 11pt

Contents

Part Four

Acknowledgements

Some of the poems in this selection have been previously published in:

Boomer, Craccum, Critic, JAAM, Metro, Other Voices 2 (ed. Bernard Gadd), *Pacific Voices: An Anthology of Maori and Pacific Writing* (ed. Bernard Gadd), *Pilgrims, Rambling Jack* (ed. Gregory O'Brien), *Samoan Observer, Saoirse, Snafu, Te Ao Marama* (ed. Witi Ihimaera), *Tiger Words, Tango* and *Whetu Moana* (eds. Robert Sullivan, Albert Wendt and Reina Whaitiri).

Apart from several previously unpublished poems, O'Leary's works from which this selection was compiled include:

Surrogate Children (Lancaster Publishing, 1981)
Ten Sonnets (Martian Way Press, 1985)
Before And After (Miracle Mart Receiving, 1987)
The Irish Annals of New Zealand (ESAW, 1991)
Noa/Nothing I (Original Books, 1997)
Con Art: Selected Poems (Original Books, 1997)
Shake Speer's Faith (Original Books, 1998)
Ka Atu I Koopua — Out of the Deep (Original Books, 1999)
T.A.B. Ula Rasa (Original Books, 2001)
Unlevel Crossings (Huia Publishers, 2002)

The poem 'He Waiatanui kia Aroha' appeared as a limited edition hand-made book printed by Brendan O'Brien in 2001.

'Flipside to the Ballad of John and Yoko' (1980, 2nd ed. ESAW, 1999) appeared as a limited edition broadsheet.

Special thanks to John Baxter, F. W. N. Wright, and to Mark Pirie for first initiating this project in 2000 after reading an earlier edition of my poems, *Con Art*.

This book is to be released in conjunction with the CD, *Toku Tinihanga*, available from ESAW Sounds Divisions, PO Box 42, Paekakariki, Aotearoa/New Zealand.

Foreword

If you like Michael O'Leary's poems, you should read his novels. If you like Michael O'Leary's novels, you should read his poems, because, in both cases, they illustrate one another, making clearer what is obscure in the other.

The poetry is always easier to read and understand than the novels are at times. But the novels tend to provide a wider framework for many of the poems. Indeed, all Michael O'Leary's writings hang together. The main links are the love poetry (waiata kia aroha) and Rubesahl, a figure derived from German folklore.

This new book of selected poems (1982-2002) represents a considerable portion of his poetry but readers are advised to read his previous volumes for those works not included here. The most demanding poem in this book is 'Shake Speer's Faith', which therefore requires extended remarks.

O'Leary's poem is a masterpiece and an indubitable epic in many respects. It is magnificently organised in structure, from the 'Prologue in Heaven' to the 'Epilogue in Hell', which of course looks back to the *Book of Job* and *Faust*.

O'Leary's poem is an epic (or at least a short epic, an epyllion) because it deals with historical figures and events. There is no doubt that even at the end of the 20th century there is great sensitivity in many quarters to treatment of Nazi personalities in any but the most disapprobatory terms. However, O'Leary is justified in epicising Nazis, because that is exactly what every epic does. Who thinks Hector and Achilles were anything but thugs? What was Aeneas? Of all the historical figures in world history the one always put on a par with Adolf Hitler is Attila the Hun, a notable character in all versions of the great Teutonic epic: the Nibelungelied.

Concern may be felt that O'Leary relates himself in the persona of Rubesahl to his historical material. However, all writers of epic involve themselves and the views of their own age in their epics. The most obvious and extreme example is Dante, but it is true of all epic writers, even Homer, who makes fun of the Olympian gods and obviously does not personally

9

share the values of his militarists. This is true though Homer was in fact a series of redactors still working on the text as late as 300 BC. That's how all the early epics developed. The Nibelungenlied author is no different from Homer in the same respects. In fact he goes for laughs even more obviously.

This poem is in the Spanish manner in respect that it is written in an adaptation of the Quintilla, in Spanish metre, a verse of five octosyllabic lines of which no three consecutive lines may rhyme together.

People may wonder why O'Leary has written his epic in such a style as he uses, one given to long involute sentences. Again this is the authentic style of epic from Homer to Dante. O'Leary feels it matches Spenser's. In fact it is much more like Shelley's. Nobody has ever been able to punctuate Shelley's verse helpfully. Indeed Shelley didn't even try, leaving it to his friends (such as Peacock, who can't be said to have succeeded). O'Leary hardly bothers with punctuation anyway. But if you attend to the text carefully you will always find at any point that O'Leary's text hangs upon some point that precedes, though it may be a few good lines before. Also remember that all epics are prosaic.

O'Leary's epic may be difficult and may never be popular, but it is the summation of themes that have run through O'Leary's fiction and poetry for 20 years. That is why it is given these extended remarks.

At times Michael O'Leary's fiction shows the influence of John Lennon's books. But the strongest influence on O'Leary's shorter poems is James K. Baxter. Such were the big influences of Michael O'Leary's youth.

O'Leary's writings in the Romantic vein carry an immense conviction. Technically Michael O'Leary's poetry shows a wide range, succeeding both without rhyme and with rhyme. His sonnets illustrate both practices. This book of poems presents the most ready approach to a powerful writer who never falls into mediocrity and consistently shows a strain of genius.

F. W. N. WRIGHT, PhD
WELLINGTON

Part One

T.A.B. Ula Rasa

and

Other Best Bets

T.A.B. Ula Rasa

Nga mohio o te tangata wairua
(the emergence of an Orakei Bastard)

Caravaggio, Michelangelo, Leonardo,
Illuminated Manuscripts, Raphael, David,
Manet, Monet, Modigliani, Picasso,
Duchamp, Rossetti — all these names meant nothing to the boy.

But as he walked through the large,
Forbidding double church doors he
Entered the world which emulated
The spirit of all the artists mentioned. In the shabby, fractured,

Flaking plaster statues and effigies
Surrounding the walls and altar
Of the suburban holy place he
Experienced the same grandeur and expectation inherent

In the approximation of the spirit
Which these artists fulfil in their
Task to bring their works of human
Suffering and joy into plastic manifestation. Every Sunday

The boy would be subjected not
Only to the dark vagaries and subtle
Hopes engendered by the canon
Of the Catholic Mass, but also his eye was given the comely

And inspirational beauty the aging,
Chipped artworks and icons presented.
As the morning sun shone through
Stained glass windows and the rays landed on the bloodstained

Open-handed Christ on the Cross
The magnificent sacrifice became
Embedded in the boy's mind as
'Artistic Vision'. Such dramatic and emblematic scenes

Held in the soul of the young boy
As he tried to make sense of his
World outside art and religion.
The struggle to comprehend the secular machinations

Of commerce and love were like
A wall of fear and ignorance
From which he retreated. His only
Consolation was that somewhere God and Artists existed,

Although they were nowhere
To be found in the Auckland
Suburban Gehenna. At night,
Lying awake in his bed in the state house of lost dreams,

He could hear the industrial
Diesel drone of a southbound
Goods train and he felt terrified
By its insistent intrusion. However, in some unspoken way

It represented the same intense
Inanity of spiritual deprivation
Which the icons of Christian
Oppression also embodied in his psyche. Across the universe

Flew sparks of the unknown
Which landed in the hearts
Of the Artists who in turn gave
Expression to the fragmentary pieces of understanding coming

From outside in the cold distance.
Uncomprehendingly acknowledging
Everything there was to know
I looked and felt the pulse of life, which is the Artist's domain.

In my unknowing innocence I could experience everything
The world had to offer. Hey Jude, don't make it bad . . .

Rubesahl

a fable in Four Parts, with a prologue and epilogue

Prologue

Mein name ist Rubesahl
For many centuries I lived on the outskirts
Of towns and villages near the Black Forest
And one of my names means Ghost of the Mountains
My dark hair and beard made me mysterious
And people would fear
And revere me
In 1944 I left my ancestral home
Haunted by the darkness and anarchy which reigned

i

I could not travel as a spirit
For the world had made me worldly
By the time I left old Germany
So I escaped in a U Boat wolf-pack

Not used to temporal confinements
And restrictions of the human body
I roamed restless from country to country
Afraid of nothing but my own fears

At nights whilst I wandered some foreign road
The moon and stars shining in my brain
My heart would be reminded of the pain
Caused by loneliness and separation

I carried the burden of guilt for my people
Though no one I met ever knew this
But there was not a woman I could kiss
And not feel that I was a deceiving Judas

ii

At the half-century I arrived as a not born baby
In the remote southern land
Nothing more than an embryo, a bland
Homunculus in my Mother's womb

I arrived early and so
Was a little unsteady on my feet
My understanding of things was incomplete
And education just confused the issue

So with a child's mind I tried
To understand why I didn't belong
Why I felt unusual, why all wrong
Amongst these foreign people, my family

Once I was playing war with other boys
And I wore the symbol of the broken cross
The swastika, I was the Kommandant, the boss
But my father told me off, saying I could be arrested

iii

Later my earth parents died
Other people tried to tie me down
But I felt threatened and thought I would drown
In the sea of human obligation

I moved southward on a journey of discovery
I went to a place which was neither here nor there
It was this strange stone city where
They told me why I didn't belong

One day I stood on a mountain
Snow was falling on the surrounding rocks
The cold went to my bones — a memory unlocks
In my mind, a vision of the Black Forest in winter

Am I evil, I wondered
And this thought drove me on like a demon
The darkness inside me fuelled the notion
I moved further away from the life around me

iv

Three women teachers came to me, old and young
Dark and light, friend and lover
With each of them I would discover
Something of myself and my loneliness

One of the three tried to awaken me as a human
You are just ordinary she said to me
For a while it is with you I want to be
But I was afraid of her words and love

The next one was my blood sister
Come on, she said, let's go brother
To find the ancient land of our father and mother
I hugged her close and said goodbye

On a windswept suburban railway platform
The old woman looked at me and said
Rubesahl, Rubesahl like a voice from the dead
And the past before the past opened up before me

Epilogue

What now for this Rubesahl
Who took on human form so he could live
Only now it is too late to return to the spirit
Rubesahl will die and alone and haunted
With the irony of love following him for eternity
His mind will be his Black Forest now
And he will fear
What he reveres
The mist closes around the Ghost of the Mountain
The mist behind which he hid for all those centuries

Shake Speer's Faith

an epyllion in the Spanish manner

Prologue in Heaven

There is a tale of two people of yore and now
Both Giants and Monsters in their own way
For whom the earth quakes when they come out to play
One born under a shroud of mountain mystery
The other from urbane and respectable beginnings

The hills and mist whence the first one comes
Hid him for many mythological years
The peasant people around the area had fears
Of this dark presence of a man, this Rubesahl
And stories of his evil doings were ever present

The other man of this epic story
Was deemed to be of the opposite demeanour
Mild of manner, no-one would have dreamed or
Thought this gentle, well-bred person
Would wield such future power over life and death

Yet, fate works in mysterious ways
And love knows no boundaries or fences
Indeed, it undermines the best made defences
Leaving exposed and vulnerable the most
Formidable and hardened battle-worn soldier

For love and fate are what this tale hangs by
Each of the two very different but the same
Each is a love which cannot speak its name
Yet, as its fires build, does not know itself
But is consumed in flames and darkness

So begins a tale of two people of now and before
Whose paths unbeknownst many times have crossed
And whose souls in destructive dark life will be lost
The only light in their lives the hopeless love
They share for dreams which can never be

Beyond the specific nature of their crimes
Lie even deeper fears of decay and corruption
Which if revealed would cause ruction
Tearing the world asunder with unknown disease
Of such thoughts of spiritual and moral depravity

In the beginning of the world was the word
Thus begins this treatise: though not anti-semantic
The cynical times in which we live appear unromantic
And worldly beyond the point of communication
Except for furiously fleeting images and ideas

Whose language and meaningless, banal ideologies
Of superficial existence reflect a wariness of ideal-ism
Idealisms which in the past, seen through a prism
Darkly, witness the mistakes of failed gods and fantasy
So we exist in a time unable to take a chance on love

Post-modern almost to the point of being post-human
For in dismissing the individual's wrongs we neglect
The ability of redemption, with typical lack of respect
We all suspect each other's dreams and motives
So there is no timc or space to reflect upon life's nature

Part the One — Rubesahl and Speer

Fateful fantasies and realities
Often of great import or moment
Are from heaven or hell sent
In the guise of imperious inspiration
Or love so strong as to tear the world asunder

Underneath such a cloak lie hidden
Temptations yet unseen and unfelt
That would make the strongest person melt
Into a mire of death and desire
Just to fulfil an unknown destiny

As so often happens at a time
Of strongest passion, death and love
Merge, so that below becomes above
The world, nay, the universe is thrown
In reverse to the way things should be

And all men, even giants and monsters,
Become as children when they are ill
No struggle, no triumph of will
At such times can overcome the constant
Undermining of life occurring from within

It is at such times thus mentioned
That the two people — both man and ghost
Will be tested by aspects of the most
Severe forms of love's infirmity
And life's infirm foundations of clay

Into the depths of underworldly life
They will both come from or dive
Both will emerge fighting and alive
Only to be drawn down again and again
By their passions and frailties

The man, the ghost of a man, of this story
Albert Speer, to many a villain
Was victim to the love of another man
Adolf Hitler, who enchanted and mesmerised
Our ante-hero into moral ambivalence

Moral ambiguity reigned in this sphere
Of the dark of twilight
So that day became night
In this realm of yes means no
Where the doctor is the Angel of Death

If work makes you free then it is true
There were many free men in this place
(Outwardly in despair and disgrace)
Enslaved by this Munitions Minister's need
To outreach production figures for his Fuhrer

One million people equalled one million units
All in black and white, accounting for a
Correct entry in the books: not even Dora
Seen through his own eyes, could shake Speer's
Resolve to get the work done at any cost

Even Himmler's own dark words spoken
Through his Death's Skull mouth at Posen
Were, by Speer, unheard and forgotten
But underneath, the black-night knowledge
Learned there created a canccrous malaise

Illness struck and laid him low
How could his 'love' have invented such destruction
Of life and love! How could his self deception
Have allowed him to go along with
And foster and profit from such evil?

And the ghost of this story who became a man
Rubesahl, to many also a villain
As love's victim, for love of a woman
Another man's wife, who enchanted
Mesmerising him into moral ambivalence

And moral ambiguity, although herself
She was a caring Christian and a pillar
Of salty society, not accepting a wife's lot, from afar
Did not look back to see the fruits
Of the tree of knowledge — or temptation falling

Rubesahl, himself a spiritual exile
From the destructive landscape which haunted
Speer's Spandau years, and daunted
By the evil of his own many centuries past
Which he tried to escape by becoming human

However, to be human is to err
And when the ghost entered real life
His strong and strange attraction for the wife
Of his best friend sent him reeling
The feeling of betrayal never far from sight

As the hazards of being human
For the ghost became more than a game
The hate which could not speak its shame
Entered his heart at every turn
Until it grew into a dark, unspeakable fear

So that he longed to return to the spirit
To shed the desires and temptation
To return to a life of contemplation
Hidden forever behind his former mantle
Of aloofness and shrouded non-involvement

Speer and Rubesahl thus were both drawn
Down into depths so deep and unknown
By magnetic passions each his own
Of opposite pulls from the separated separate
Loves which drove their lives like some demonic engine

Both Rubesahl and Speer lived in a state of 'Lebensluge'
Each of their lives was a living lie
But neither openly asked the question, why?
Which tormented their dreams and sleep
Forcing them further towards disaster by day

Part the Two – Speer

Born into solid privilege and money
Albert Speer was a delicate child
While all his siblings displayed wild
Unruly childlike behaviour, Albert was
Always the shy-looking one in family portraits

Initially, the youngster appeared average
Gifted, yet of no significant talent
His teenage years came and went
With nothing more remarkable than
An interest in the rude health of the outdoors

His shy, retiring nature meant he was
Cut off from normal social intercourse
In fact, the only real intimate source
Of communication was his developing and
Frowned-upon relationship with his future wife

Margaret, the girl from the wrong side of the tracks
And more importantly, her family
Provided the young Speer with a place he could be
Himself, without the pretence and pseudo-aristocratic
High society of his own people

So cut off from his mother and father
Had he become, that when he and his betrothed
Married, his own parents didn't even know
The young man and his bride exiling themselves
Into the lakes and mountains for several weeks

Thus at the launching pad of his career
This young man, Albert Speer, stood like millions
Of his generation in uncertainty — his opinions
Unformed, waiting for someone or something
To provide a source of worth and belonging

The turbulent times of Germany in the Twenties
And Thirties meant, coupled with the usual
Ferment of teenage years in the pursual
Of 'The Meaning of Life' is desperately sought
By the young, that normal search was intensified

At the behest of his student friends
The doubting Speer attended a political rally
Until this time he had treated equally
All politics with distance and disdain
In fact, it never even entered his consciousness

Expecting to see the maniacal media image
Instead, Hitler took the podium wearing a suit
And in low, modulated tones, not the brute
Force portrayed so oft, he spoke in measured
Intelligent language of his dreams for the future

Our anti-hero, Speer, the sensitive student
Was stunned into silence and respect
Not by what the speaker said, but the direct
Pierce of pure intensity and passion which radiated
From the look in the eyes of his future Fuhrer

So, from that day forward until doubt set in
Late in the war, Hitler totally mesmerised
With his unique personality and his eyes
Whose look captured the young Albert's heart
And also that of a whole beguiled nation

In those early innocent, heady days
There were humorous incidents, yes
Speer became a member of the murderous S.S.
Only because he was wealthy enough to own
A car, and he could fit the "Sultan's" hat

And unbeknownst to him at this early stage
His mother had also secretly joined the Party
When each found out they had a good hearty
Laugh together, perhaps the only intimate moment
They had shared in their estranged relationship

Under Hitler's patronage once the Nazis took power
Speer's career as an architect flourished
His aims and ambitions were nourished
By such triumphs as the 'Cathedral of Light'
And his prizewinning design at the Paris World Fair

So engrossed was Speer in his leader's plans
He neglected his personal life almost completely
The architect of false dreams in fact only
Became a father, not because of love of his wife
But, because Hitler suggested it was the right thing

Almost like a metaphor for his generation
Speer could not see the dark, sinister clouds
Gathering of war and destruction, only the crowds
Whose strength was attained through the joy
Of serving their beloved Reich and Saviour

And with the war came the early victories
Blindly the people celebrated the successes
Turning the other cheek to rumours of excesses
The only things they wanted to know
Were what their Fuhrer chose to tell them

Prepared by propaganda now to accept any outrage
Or atrocity, the unearthly cry 'No Jews is Good Jews'
Became the daily, unspoken-of news
In a country once heralded as the leading light
Of civilisation, art and cultural thought

At the centre of the gathering maelstrom
Stood Speer, no longer an artist but the Minister
Of Armaments and War Production, an administrator
Determining the fate and future of millions
No longer the creator of dreams but of death

It is at this pinnacle of personal power, with Speer
Struggling to forget things which cannot be forgotten
Things spoken of by the Reichsfuhrer S.S. at Posen
It is at this great height from which he falls
Into physical illness caused by moral amnesia

Part the Three — Rubesahl

The mortal failings of this immortal demigod
And the mysterious mist surrounding his life
From beneath which he so loved the wife
Of another man, he gave away his soul
To the void of inverted Mephistophelian eternity

But even darker forces are beckoned forth
From the past before the past, which reveals
Ever darkening hints of demonic deals
Struck, even before his birth on earth
Yea, in the spirit world of the ancient and lost

His story down all the days and years
Historically the facts of which often meant
He had to cover his tracks, or indeed invent
Tales so outrageous that even his intimates
Of many years did not know who he was

Seemingly born into humble beginnings
His young years spent in relative poverty
So that so-called 'normal' youth was a novelty
To this State House boy, left uncultured
Uneducated and unequiped for the temporal world

Also, he was born with the mark of Satanic sign
Like a palsy he carried as though it were a lover
Whenever he tried to lose it, he could not cover
This mark of destiny which other children laughed at
Calling him names and making him feel ashamed

So he grew up, more like some weird, wayward
Plant, than the cultivated suburban houseplants
His contemporaries, who followed the smooth advance
Of school, work, university and/or marriage
Rubesahl became lost in the misty mystery of fate

When as a child he played at war with his
School friends, he would always be the baddie —
The underdog, the Indians, and significantly,
The Germans — he, it was noted by those around
Him, liked particularly to wear the swastika

His father and his mother, in the earthly sense
Had their fair share of troubles and frustration
One of their daughters died, and in exasperation
At their penniless existence, the father stole money
From his boss which meant he ended up in jail

Whilst in his lonely incarceration he wrote
Letters to his even more lonely wife, Rubesahl's mother
Revealing many unspoken of things leading her to discover
That her husband, in fact, blamed God
For their child's death, indeed a terrible revelation

For devoutly Catholic people know too well
The penalties for sinning against the creator —
Being brought up as a Catholic sooner or later
Appears like a Disneyland where everything is painted
Black, and the guilt-edged life must come to an end

It was not too long before both his parents died
And he, the young Rubesahl, went to work in
A dark, thankless factory where amidst the unholy din
And noise of making stove elements by the thousand
He sought escape and beauty in dreams of dreams

He began to feel restless and humiliated
By his 'imprisonment', kept captive in a menial task
His mind questioned why he had to be there, and to ask
Beyond the confines of his workaday world
Why and what were his strange visions of not belonging?

For all his life, ever since he could remember
Rubesahl lacked a sense of belonging
To his siblings, to his country, he felt on ongoing
Detachment, as though he was from far away
Elsewhere, a place more ominous than these sunshine shores

So the young man of ghosts cut himself adrift
Travelling aimlessly around the country of his birth
From North Cape to Bluff, and across each island's girth
Drunk, always drunk, on whiskey, poetry and vice
A deadly combination of potent self-destruction

In the unfathomable depth of despair
One day a light shone, piercing the black
Hole of his mind's gutter, reaching his lack
Of closeness to others, thus Rubesahl glimpsed
Beyond the borders of his sunless world

Through the unexpected quarter of his friend's wife
Rubesahl, for a moment which was only brief
Was relinquished from his sorrow and grief
Transformed to a realm of beauty and wonder
By the voice and touch of one who seemed untouchable

The weary wisdom of the world is never far away
And our joys soon turn to sadness, our laughter to tears
Rubesahl, in finding this place of solace, now bears
An even deeper driven exile than before as he
Struggles with sin of where his passion led

Betrayal of trust, treading the fine line of false
Hypocrisy and friendship, making untruthful claims
To facilitate and validate his unscrupulous aims
The world had indeed made him worldly and devious
As he became lost in his dark and dangerous love

A child was born, not to her but to her namesake
For his purity of spirit could no longer withstand
His outbursting of uncontrollable grief and
Inconsolable longing for a love which could never be
Of this world, although his dreams and spirit disagreed

So that at the height of his personal desires
Rubesahl struggled to forget the unforgettable one
By taking to his bed another — what's done is done!
And in his new attempt to belong he now falls
Into physical illness caused by moral turpitude

Part the Four — Speer and Rubesahl

As the men lay in their hospital beds dying
Both Speer and Rubesahl had out-of-body experiences
During which they died and everything made sense
Their hallucinatory states invoked an image of reality
And both were returned to life to complete their tasks

When Doctor Brandt came to diagnose Speer
He could detect not just political, but also personal drama
"Certainly not due to a physical trauma"
He proclaimed in an aside to the Reichminister's aide
Not entirely caused by Himmler's plotting either

'All men, even giants, become childish when ill'
Thus Rubesahl from this offhand proclamation
Recognised a profound insight about his destination
Which hinted to him of his former self
As he deliriously rambled childlike

In his dream-like state he remembered well
How, as his spirit left Germany in darkness
In 1944, he touched the spirit of another in distress
And gently bade it return to its temporal palace
Its sphere on earth, where it still had a part to play

And at Rubesahl's bidding Speer returned, the same
Yet changed beyond recognition, for he now
Saw Hitler and his dreams differently somehow
As his face now displayed distortion and ugliness
So his desires and aspirations now appeared disastrous

But as with Rubesahl's latter day return to forbidden
Thoughts of love of that which is unallowable
Speer too was soon back in an unavowable
Self deception as he set to work ever harder
To win a war which could never be won

Rubesahl, too, was sent backwards reeling
With the remembrance of things past
After his own recovery he looked aghast
At himself walking down the aisle of the cathedral
At a funeral, not a wedding, but with her by his side

He felt so in love as they sang together
In unison, like at the marae not long before
At the scene of a tangi which had been more
Tragic — we are all together at times of love
And death, as it was for ghost and his neverlove

Yet, every time he had to leave her, yes, every time
They parted, he felt a gap widening in his soul
Where fearful visions filled the vacant hole
She left, the terror he had of being alone and
Of his being exposed for his crimes which he knew

Or suspected he knew: so it was the same for Speer
Both men's illnesses had been their response to doubt
The essential link between them — fear of being found out
Thus they shared Himmler's sacred realm of dream
Reality, like any other demon haunter of the human race

Yet, how can be equated the sins and misdemeanours
Of a chief architect and planner of the monstrous Third Reich
Who, with his Fuhrer turned light to dark, day to night
Who, despite his suit and tie, his attention to duty
Sent unwittingly or otherwise, millions to their death

With the seemingly minor mortal sin of adulterous thoughts,
Words, and indeed, intention – a sordid, yet common crime
The link is the shared humanity extant throughout time
That we all fall short of the glory of perfection is true
And we must live with what we do and the consequences

Whether it be Speer's brother, Ernst, who visited
His famous older sibling (who couldn't make time for him)
Only days before being posted to the Russian Front, where grim
And bitter he cursed Albert as he lay wounded and dying
In the mud and filth and freezing horrors of Stalingrad

Or, whether it is the mother of Rubesahl's fatherless child
Who daily lives with his cares and concerns
Feeling herself neglected, such knowledge burns
Like a smouldering fire as she remembers the time
They were together, yet not really together at all

And Rubesahl also reflects and he remembers too
The old Jewish woman, who on an Auckland Suburban
Railway platform pointing her finger at him in an
Unfamiliar, humorous, yet accusing manner, saying
"Rubesahl! Rubesahl!" — like she knew who he really was

That old woman knew all the sorrows of the world
Her entire family perished in Hitler's Holocaust
She escaped, but married a 'Kiwi' who, at best
Treated her worse than any Nazi inspired pogrom
As all her windswept dreams were shattered

Similar fingers of judgement and accusation
Were pointed again and again at Albert Speer
Whose specific knowledge was neither here nor there
Of Posen or of Dora, or of any cruelty or killing
But, he was a willing participant in the general melee

And, Rubesahl too was there, although he did get out
In a U Boat wolf-pack when he could finally see
The mayhem and anarchy caused by the deadly spree
Of the artists and other misfits who unleashed their
Drunken bohemian corporeal orgy of power and destruction

Thus, the moral ulcer of inaction festered
Deep in the hearts of these two men of talent
Even when Speer attempted to kill Hitler, he went
To poison the Fuhrerbunker's air vents, but felt
Relieved when he realised they had been moved

And Rubesahl, now far away from his ill-fated
Lover, still feels her hold as she recently tested
His resolve when her mother died. She re-arrested
His heart and resurrected his desire for the closeness
He only ever got from her, at the midnight Railway Station

Epilogue — In Hell

As in his cloistered haven, Spandau, Speer walked
Around the world, so did Rubesahl's spirit roam
Looking, both of them, for that elusive home
Where one can be at peace, and the struggle to be
Is left well and truly outside the world's door

Both describe their long and arduous isolation
As though it had set them free, like some scene
In a movie. Hitler and Rubesahl's love had been
The agents of that freedom and tranquillity
Which, when reversed and lost was sorely felt

And both would nearly embrace death as a solution
For their pain of the knowledge of good and evil
Death, whose finality, or so it seems, will
Take away the suffering of moral quandaries
Leaving the recipient free in eternal annihilation

But despite the seemingly easy end of suicide
To that struggle for truth and just to survive
Although both chose reckless, dangerous lives
In essence both believed in life enough
Not to lay down and surrender to the void

Rubesahl, who chose mortal, human existence
And in times past flew on wings of desire
Became and gave allegiance to the passionate fire
Of life on earth, for had he remained simply a spirit
He would have always seemed a spectre of fear

And Speer, the quiet dreamer of great buildings
Who became detested from elements of left and right
Whose 'mea culpas' at Nuremberg did not sound quite
Honest, yet were enough to save his life
So he could live long enough to inform us
Of the great tragedy which he experienced from inside

Not only the Third Reich, but also his personal
Depths, his knowledge of the battle of Heaven and Hell
Which rages incessantly inside all of us to see
Who gains ultimate control over our eternal souls

This is the point on which this tale hinges
It is with these problems each of us must wrestle
There is no safe house, no illusory nest for us to nestle
In, away from the great war which ever rages
The struggle through the ages for some homecoming

Which we may or may not achieve in life or death
In Speer and in Rubesahl, as in all humanity
The measure of their dreams where all is vanity
Is their innocence, which almost destroyed them
Unaware, as they were, of their potential to destroy

So, the cycle of life turns yet further onwards
Grinding well beyond historical inevitability
As each turn of the wheel reveals a new vulnerability
Enabling us to see, through each person's story
The fight with themselves to discover the unknowable

Walter Pater stripped bare by his bachelors even

(a ready-made poem for Hone Tuwhare
and everybody else in the goddam world!!!)

Doo wop, doo wop, doo chomp, chomp, chomp
Mmmmmmmmmmmmm, luverly lufting snow
Through the swirling Berlin Strasse we clomp
Clomp, clomp — Deaf Ted, Danoota and Primo
Without a hint of the usual Teutonic pseudo-pomp

How can a ready-maid rhymegold so easily!!!
          You may well arske, and why?
Well if it's . . . enough for Gaston de Latour
It's . . . enough for me and Bobby Tuwhare
So, wot are ya on (about)
Three holes in the ground — I'll tell you
Now, the walrus was he!
Johny Lee Lewisham (forget the fish)
Moondogs baying for blut: ie, what the 'Heroes' of the
Renaissance
Created on marble cliffs
And on canvas, with hammers
And chisels or paint
Brush with paint and shaved ham
Fisting the knight away (somewhere uppa New York way)
Cook up a samwitch, thus a Budheist treat
(Re; one with everything). Hey! On rye, thanks Mack.

Then sculpted in form from the bland
Wordless page with which he began
Using his inner eye to guide his hand
Pater builds rather a word picture than
An ordinary, everyday image — a grand
Frontis connecting the 'finesse of sensation'
To Montaigne and his 'two great affections'

Part Two

The 'Kia Aroha' Poems

Kia Aroha

Listening to a poet reading poetry
Was the small flicker of flame
Which lit this poem in my heart

When he, with another woman in mind,
Mentioned a furcoat-wrapped woman
Your image leapt at me, is now here to stay

I have carried you all day with me
Through the hard-nosed life of a labouring man
Your beauty is so strong that I weep inward

Yet, like your Master's kingdom,
Our love cannot be of this world
You exist for me as He does for you

And your husband and your children
Stand between us like trees against the horizon
At the point of sundown and the rising darkness
                                        I see you

Kia Aroha — rua

we sat silent at the foot
of the poet's statue
I had put my coat around you
to keep off the southern evening coldness
and, with my arm around your shoulder
we waited in the Octagon
for the time we would no longer be together

which came soon enough —
as your husband's car came to a stop
at the traffic lights
my arm moved instinctively away
and the seeds of the trees
which necessarily separate us
are again planted

but each time
we are apart we grow together
like an unseen river
beneath the surface of our lives
the aroha
is between us
as well as the distance

and that evening
we had laughed and danced, sang
and talked of death and darkness and light
the best thing was that we were happy
as we walked from the restaurant
to sit silent at the foot
of the poet's statue

Kia Aroha – toru

to describe thoughts and feelings
  these in reality have already gone
what is left that lingers on
  in fact has only just begun
the love that dares not speak
  can only whisper
  small, soft words
like fingers half touching
telling of a longing
  to understand

in the night
  by the fireside
bright sparks and gentle flames
  bring warmth and light
the manuka took so long to grow
  soon burns
  adding to our inner glow
the mystery deepens
the pain I am left with
recedes into darkness

Kia Aroha — wha

it is the possibilities —
the first feelings of being human
                             and beyond . . .
the unbridgeable gulf and
deadly separation
caused by the original sin,
wilful knowledge of good and evil,
. . . love heals these deep wounds
in our soul,
understanding the depths and heights
to which we go

the river through
which we drag each other
and the beauty which lightens us
as we share each other's
touch and grace,
the embrace that sends electric currents
through our bodies comes from the ancient
impulse to belong . . .
we dare not hold on too long,
we dare not let go . . .

Kia Aroha — rima

(a fragment, a dream: he moemoea, no reira)

The two angels turned
And facing each other
Became wooden ancestors
Standing together across the marae atea

He with his ure proud, erect
And constant until being, centuries later,
Emasculated with the Missionary
Position on such obvious love

And her breasts were covered
Painted over rather than cut off
But, still her womanhood
Somehow lessened by dear prudence

Ano, these two kaitiaki o aroha
Whose love was carved out
So long ago will now
Heal their wounds, uncover their wairua
                         their mauri
                              Ka mate, ka mate
                              ka ora, ka ora

Kia Aroha — ono

(Mini Joko Haiku)

To force your hand, I
Had to draw or repel you
— a no Win solution

He Waiatanui kia Aroha

i

twilight falls
among the large stone buildings
grey monoliths — but undemanding
to the modern eye
as we walked towards the taxi
I stopped and wanted to kiss you
And you said maybe
        then we did kiss
holding our mouths together like beaks
        but sweet, ambiguous even
and I shuddered with emotion
        my whole being shook
        with the physical knowledge
        of our parting . . .

ii

        before we had met that evening
I had felt the fear and longing
of anticipation
— the uncertainty of what to feel
I sat in a café and drank slowly
a cool glass of orange
watching you
on the other side of the road
for a few moments
as you watched and waited
for signs of me
— then I drained
        the remaining liquid
        from the glass . . .

iii

I took your arm as we walked
to our meeting eating place
our time out to be together place
where time goes in split seconds
so that an hour seems a minute
      is gone too soon and forever
and out is what happens
      at the end of time . . .
      but those precious moments
we are there, in our time capsule,
make up for all our partings
      because I know what it's like
      to be without you . . .
All the years of wanting you
      have softened me up
      have made me sensitive
to the moments we are together
so that I treat each one
      like a treasure: taurite he taonga . . .

iv

you apologised for crying
(about your family) as we talked
      don't apologise to me, Winsome,
you have probably not given
      a show of emotion
(I was going to say weakness —
but I meant vulnerability)
      private or public, too often
but I have cried openly
for the want of you
for the fact that we must be apart
- so don't apologise to me . . .

v

twilight brings
its gradual descent of the night
on Seacliff
and the sea and
the clouds touch
merge into one blue-grey hue . . .
as with the sky
and the land
the trees turn ever darkening
shades of green
the last remaining residue
of crimson
is stretched, elongated
diffuse across the horizon
and these seen things
are mirrored within
as my thoughts of you
are repeated over and over
ever changing
ever increasing with the days
the same subtle blend as landscape
of colours and shapes
sometimes clearly defined
sometimes barely discernible
and sometimes
the darkness is complete

vi

the incomplete nature of our beings
and the knowledge
glimpsed at through you
of what we need
to bridge that
separation . . .

vii

the light beyond the horizon
      is te Marama
      who, when she shines
      touches the silent, sleeping
      soul of the earth
it is this unseen world
alive with the light
      of the unknown
where my love for you
      lies waiting —
beyond those tall trees
that rising darkness
and sensuous sundown
of strange, stark colours
te po, te po, te po aroha
      the moonlight world
      of our understanding
      the Polynesian darkness
      of light . . .

viii

the other day
we met
      in a public way —
friends talking
a hongi
      and a kiss
from a girl
      who said you were too much for her
so much so
that she had to go
      (followed by dreadlocks, himself)
and the bond between us
couldn't help itself
as we embraced with a passion
and stood holding hands
— despite all that was around us

ix

the evil within me
which struggles for possession
of my mind and soul
in the ancient attempt
to bring me down
as it has done for generations
before and after me
      is quelled
by my responsibility to you

x

later I heard your telephone voice
full of the cares of domesticity
but still sweet
and coming from deep
within our history
so that despite the aloofness
and separateness
I sometimes feel
from your life
there is always a place
      at which we touch

xi

the candlelight flickered
and I was half in a dream
— more like a feeling of missing
  you and not knowing you
I stepped outside
and there the moon was rising
like the tip of a lightberg
shining through the dense
cloud cover
and I thought

                    this is how I know you
                    distant
                            with slowly
                                    evolving revelation . . .
I am trying to think of you
I am trying to imagine
            what you look like
            and all I can do
            is feel your absence
            like a mystery waiting to be solved
I cannot be near you
at our Timeout of the month
and the full moon is hiding behind the rain
(the tears of Rangi, e Papa)
the sky is filled with separation
the horizon is the natural split
between (the sea) the earth and the sky
but there is no split
            because there is
                        no touching

   xii

            a picture of you
            looks up, smiling
            and connects me
to the world of feelings
the deep questions of life and
love and eternity
which have had their evocation so often
                through you
you are my point
of contact with life, yet
you are so distant and yet again
that distance is
                broken
as the fine fibre of love you weave around me
                tightens — it is
the dynamics of something set in motion
rather than necessarily an act of consciousness

the earth is sleeping
dreams are walking around, entering
each heart, each body —
each soul is enchanted either by dreams
or nightmares haunting the darkness
with ever greater darkness
                    te ua, te ua, nga roimata ahau
                    te haunui o te wairua
                    te ariki o te ao
and in the beginning was the word . . .

xiii

wrapped in a blanket
I sit and listen
to the wind blow
hard out along the coast
whipping up the water
scraping and shaping the land —
sending chunks of sure cliffs
crashing to the sea below . . .
cold wind was always
the worst to work in
sapping energy from my body
even before the first shovel-load
had been lifted from the earth
taurite nga moehewa o Aroha . . .
but now the wind has dropped
perhaps it will wait —
then picking up my words
Te Hau will carry them
soaring southwards
over the dark hills
taking them gently
kia Aroha, down the valley
where they will reach you
as a whisper . . .

In North East Valley

Your milk splashed up into my face
Tasting warm, moist, slightly insipid

Not sweet like the milk of a coconut
But of the same tangy texture

It was your farewell gift to me
A koha that stayed all day on my tongue

Later, on the northbound train, I thought of you
And couldn't help but laugh to myself

The way you held your beautiful brown breast
Squirting at me like a child's water pistol

Now I'm a thousand miles away from you
Our lives are probably back to normal

But today the Auckland rain splashed on my face
It looked milky-white and reminded me of you

Scarf

Black and white
Hides the colours of the spectrum
Of our aroha

Defiled and soiled
Humiliated even, it slipped out, evil
Between the realm

Forever lost
It had been like a rainbow prism
A symbol

An archetype
Now like a wounded, gentle beauty
Leaving no colour

Black and white . . .

On the Death of your Mother

That morning I woke up and I put around
My neck the black and white scarf
Which several years ago I stole from your house
As a close memento of you to wear

I had not worn this, my favourite scarf,
For many moons so I knew something was afoot
When Des came running by the Raumati shops
Not a place I'm normally at on Saturday morning

And told me that your mother had died less
Than an hour before I felt the scarf tighten
The surprise was no surprise, this is the way
We are, bound together but we must be apart

I spoke to your father and gave him my aroha
And I tried to contact you and others all day
All were travelling to or from somewhere
All were out of touch through their journeys and grief

When you rang me in the late evening, saying
You needed my car to take you home to Whanganui
I felt neutral, even aloof, just waiting for the deluge
Of thoughts and feelings which I knew would come

I met you off the train at Paekakariki Station at midnight
And when we walked arm in arm along the platform
That closeness and aroha I have only found with you
Rekindled like embers left sleeping overnight

I kissed you goodbye and realised a fulfilled destiny
The reason why I had bought a car at all
Many years ago, had in my mind, been for you
And now, when you needed it, it was here

It all fitted so neatly like a fate unknown
Until its revelation, which is then shown
To be so simple, and openly mocks us
So deceptive and beguiling that it shocks us

I didn't need to go to the marae to farewell your mother
As I had planned: my role was yet again to support you
        I cannot hold you . . .
So I take off the scarf till the next time we say goodbye

Us at the Funeral of John Patrick Kennedy, 1994

The great batlike Cathedral
arms wide open
        for an embrace
        and your face
        looking flushed and radiant
as we entered from Smith Street . . .
        the physical anatomy of a church
        became an engulfing of us . . .
Memories of many people
        and of our own two memories
        the children you went to school with
        unseen these many years
        stand here now to bury their father
Those long white stone columns
        like pillars of salt
        are like my love for you
        as the choir sings
        the tunes and rhythms of death
There is so much life and love in me
        that I want to burst apart
        run screaming down the aisle
        with sheer happiness
The priests put on a great show
        their jewelled gowns
        glittering with the pathos
        of mercy and forgiveness
God knows we all need these
        small sacraments
        to keep us from going wild and insane
        the host is lifted on high
familiar rituals to me
alien rituals to you
and you understand only when I whisper
to you that it's just like the Marae

As the widow speaks of the life together
            she shared with the man who
            lies in the coffin
            I think of the separation
            of life which I must share with you
Although I am sad
            I have never been happier
            in my life as we
            exit from
            the great Gothic wings
            opening towards Otago Harbour
            into the daylight and
            talk to the people of the past
present
            at this funeral
love and death are with us . . .

Part Three

Sonnets

Songs

Satires

Sonnet for a child

Such small hands, ten small fingers, I can't see
As they fold like night flowers over my eyes
Covering my view of already dark Dunedin skies
We walk along the city streets: your mother, you and me

Up on my shoulders you're higher than the tall
You say that you can see more than all of us
"Look Mum!" you cry, "a train! a truck! a bus!"
Safe with my strength you know you will not fall

Amelia, I know you love me dearly
And I love you who have given me so much
A smile from you has often eased my heavy mind

Such pleasures I have felt with you, I have felt rarely
For I have been long alone, thus out of touch
With simple love: I'd forgotten what I set out to find

Sarah

Sarah, I see the beauty of the world
In your eyes as I hold you above me

I feel the shame of my dark-edged life
But then hear the joy of your shrill cry

As I swiftly bring you down in my arms
Just missing the prickle patch by inches

Up again you fly, this time high
Out over a ditch and we both laugh

Then back down to earth and it's time
To go: back to the city, back to myself

Now, if I sometimes feel leaden
A heavy, unmoving, lifeless thing

I remember when Sarah and I flew
She in my arms, I in her spirit

Only a Poem

In the large shadow of Lion Rock
I stood alone watching the breakers

Rolling across the horizon from the ocean
The moonlight and the cloud-cover conspired

To flood my mind with memories and
I longed to be part of you again

It was my turn to drown as you
Had drowned two hundred years ago in Upolu

When I an Irish sea captain, you a Samoan girl
Stood for awhile in passion and in fear

But, my love, your courage is that much stronger
Than mine, and the sea rolled on and on

So I stand on the shore of our love
Unable to write poetry, only poems

Sonnet to My Father

Fifteen years now since you
Gave away the struggle to live

Fifteen years since the earth yawned
And you fell in the gaping mouth

Now that I am double the age of your death
And more, now I can look back at you

You, the one who loved my mother
So that she could give life to me

From you I get my lack of security
You handed me down the keys of danger

The shadows which haunt my dreams
Are visited upon me from your demons

Fifteen years of misunderstanding you
Unless I hurry I'll never know who I am

Saturday Night

(for Patrick)

I have been drunk! On each of Baudelaire's
Fancy wings have I flown.
On wine, poetry, and the tail-wing of virtue
Have I in drunken chariots gone.

Drink! Drink! Drink! With the nebulous goal,
To find the limitless mind and soul.
On! On! On! Through light, time, and sound
Too late! I fall to the ground.

Which I hit with a terrible smash
And as a Phoenix, turn to ash.
You ask, "Like the bird
Will you rise again soon?"
I answer, "Yes, Sunday, Monday,
Or maybe Tuesday afternoon!"

Samoan Sonnet

Two hundred years since I, an Irish sea captain
With bearded face, sailed into Upolu

I saw you there in the sand Samoan girl
And the passion rose within my breast

At that time of still undiscovered voyages
We were almost lovers by the sea which took you

You drowned and I wept like a river
Then sailed home to a solitary life

Now, two hundred years later, we have met again
In the suburbs of a South Sea city

The passion rose through the complexities
Through the modern mind's menagerie of split confusion

In this age of no-adventure comfort
We embark on a still undiscovered voyage

Sonnet written upon reading Selection 14 of Dr. Johnson's 'The Rambler'

Oftentimes in the ruminous past have I wondered
Upon the amusing question of why I am a poet
Was I born with insight sublime, or did I grow it
Like some ever creeping vine my mind wandered

Wandered by day and by night, away from normal
Established thoughts and sensibilities into a jungle
Where wild, viper-like ideas merge in a tangle
Of insane ravings called poems when put in a journal

Self-cast into the wilderness, an intellectual ambler
No noise and needs of children or love of a wife
Alone, all alone! No job, like an ordinary bloke
In odious dejection I read the Doctor's 'Rambler'
In which he instructs, even then, was a poet's life
Embarrassed with obstructions, clouded in smoke

Passing Young's Lane

As the early morning train pulls out
Of Newmarket Station it dives down towards Auckland

Towards another working day: the bells ring
And the warning lights flash at Young's Lane

I look indifferently out the window
Expecting to see nothing other than dark-grey skies

To my right a shaft of golden light
Transforms the otherwise sullen landscape

Beyond the marshes and swamps of Orakei
Straight down the Gulf I see Waiheke

Where you two moved to the other day
Waiheke is the place where the light is strongest

Suddenly the train lurches to the left
We enter the Parnell Tunnel plunged into darkness

Gulls at Paekakariki

Like a welcoming committee they came
To lay down their challenge of greeting

As we sat on the rocks that overlook
The swelling surf of the beach below

Breaking open our packets of fish and chips
Had the magical attraction of a magnet

As if by internal instinct each individual
Bird performed, a form of balletic beauty

Each inspired by the proximity of the others
Who in turn tuned in to some ancient call

And took the sky, letting the wild wind guide
Their twisting and turning on tides of air

The myriad dance of daring and delight
Left us speechless at this ordinary miracle

Four Elizabethan Sonnets

1 - Lady Die

So, the hapless Lady Di is cast into eternity
By seven horsemen of the apocalyptic paparazzi
Who, like a blinded, blinkered, ideal-driven nazi
Carried out the ultimate work of their fraternity

But beneath their crazed pursuit a deeper need
Is exposed. For they were like the harbinger
Of someone to come, the maligned messenger
Whose news satisfies the masses' insatiable greed

And beyond the sentiment thus far expressed
(the ugliness of the world needing sacrificial beauty)
Lies an even darker hint of something sinister
An unsanctioned, unlawful love remains unblessed
After living lives of ostensible honour and duty
Adulterous Charles and Camilla now call the Minister

2 - The Common Touch

So, she had the common touch after all
Dying in that most egalitarian way
'Out of it' on the drink or drug of the day
The car slammed into the road-tunnel wall

Rich kids, poor kids — all on a Saturday night
No matter what your wealth or status is
Whether you're drinking D.B. or bubbly fizz
Behind the wheel you know you're all right

And the paparazzi devils who follow our lives
Haunting and taunting our most personal places
Exposing the Dorianic double nature of our lives
Determine who gets the chop and who survives

Within you and without you death is all the same
But if you're rich you can afford to apportion blame

3 - The Colonels' Plot

The inner-circular ruling lights
Of the British Defence forces
Were having sleepless nights
Counting legless Royal horses

Their cousins, the arms industry
Nervous at the Princess of Wales'
Quixotic and relentless try
To eradicate land mine sales

Losing money and losing status
Invoking their hymn and scripture
"Recruit the paparazzi to help us
She'll soon be given the picture"

What happened next, now we all know is history
The unspeakable caught the edible to cover a mystery

4 - Pomp and Grandeur

The ironic nature of her funeral cannot be stressed
Too much: as her cortege passed all she had touched
Each individual's thoughts can only be guessed
Remembering that spirit who couldn't be crushed

Locked away for years in a loveless marriage
Latterly escaping to become Queen of Hearts
The champion of peace — riding in a gun carriage
Diana, in a shortened life played many parts

The hunter was the hunted, the haunting the haunted
The fair beauty became the dark lady of this sonnet
All that wealth, health and happiness was taunted
By the devilish double-edged shadow which fell on it

That beautiful London day when millions held their breath
All that pomp and grandeur just hid another hideous death

As a Soldier

The wind blows cold in the night
Reminding me I am alone

As a soldier in a foreign land
Finds himself on an open road

He cannot read the signposts there
Nor understand people he meets

Separated after the bombardment
He no longer knows friend or enemy

Danger is his only companion
It is with him in the shadows

Love does not know who he is
But he has no time to weep

So, here the wind blows hard tonight
Reminding me I am alone

Songs

(recorded and performed by
Dunedin Irish Band, Blackthorn)

1 - Potatoes, Fish and Children

To escape from the famine, starvation and pain
And seeing his dear ones dying
Patrick Fitzgerald left old Erin's Isle
And headed for the South Seas sailing

He landed here without a pig or a bob
And decided to join the army
Because it was the only job
To take the land from the Maori

CHORUS . . .
> *He thinks to himself by the fire at night*
> *I don't know why we kill them*
> *O, sure they're the same as the people at home*
> *Potatoes, fish and children*

His orders were clear to set up a fight
So the crown could claim confiscation
Of land to which they had no legal right
By the treaty which founded the nation

As Paddy thought of it more and more
He could see that this land grabbing was not need
But just like at home in Ireland
They were killing for profit and greed

CHORUS . . .

Then one winter when the cloud hung low
And the moon was hidden by mist and by damp
He picked up his gun and some food in a sack
And crept silently out of the soldiers' camp

He travelled by night and he rested by day
To escaped from the pay of the crown
He woke up by the winter moon risin'
And went to sleep when the moon went down

CHORUS . . .

The beauty he saw in this wonderful land
Reminded him of his far away home
He fell asleep for a very long time
And he dreamed that he was no longer alone

The tribe that found him took his body back
From te wahi moemoea and restored him to life
For they saw in his eyes when they opened
Potatoes fish and children

CHORUS . . .

2 - Twilight City

The twilight comes quickly
Among the old buildings
Which to the modern eye
Stand grey and undemanding

The shadows of the city lengthen
Drawing our line of separation
Then the night comes cold and dark
Without an invitation

CHORUS . . .

> *Then it's our time to part*
> *I feel the searing of my heart*
> *As it tears asunder with the pain*
> *My tears fall down like rain*
> *My tears fall down like rain*

But when we are together
Holding hands and talking so sweet
The flow of life runs through me
And I feel like I am complete

Then I forget about walls and buildings
In your eyes is the sky and the ocean
My spirit's alive with the secrets of life
From your touch and your emotion

CHORUS . . .

But the twilight falls
It's time for you to leave me
And the gold edge to my life is gone
As the darkness comes to retrieve me

And just like the old city
Ancient and made of stone
My heart is like granite
When you leave me alone

CHORUS . . .

3 - Just Like a Bird

Candlelight flickered, I was half in a dream
As the moon rose through clouds over the bay
You came to me like a light on a beam
Now your image is with me to stay
At the end of this long working day

CHORUS . . .

> *Just like a bird*
> *My words will fly to you*
> *Across the dark and stormy waters*
> *High over hills, down the valleys below*
> *Where they'll reach you as a whisper*
> *Just like a bird*

As once I held you close in my arms
Tonight I hold you in my memory
The thought of your touch even warms the chill winds
Which sap the strength from my body
In this place where I'm working so lonely

CHORUS . . .

Sometimes I call you on the phone
The words we say bring us together again
Hearing your voice reflecting my own
I feel such sweet melancholy pain
Then the coins run out, leaving me alone again

CHORUS . . .

The only fear I have in this life
Is that I will never see you again
So hold me in you heart tonight
My love, as I sit in the darkness
When the candlelight flickers, I see you again

CHORUS . . .

4 - Southerners Crossing

Train pulled out of the old stone station
Followed the line north along the coast
It was in the long dark tunnel
That I first thought I saw your ghost

The haunting image then joined our journey
Staying with the train until the light of day
The movement and the motion just like the ocean
I knew that you were here to stay

CHORUS . . .
> *We were travelling together*
> *Although I was travelling on my own*
> *You were there beside me all the way*
> *But everyone could see I was on my own*
> *Yes everyone could see I was alone*

First time I saw you was from your carriage
Many years before this recent travel
When first our two trains stopped for each other
But where we go now only time will tell

We share the same lines in this life
But, time nor train waits for no one
Relentless movement to our separate fates
Means we can never be as one

CHORUS . . .

5 - The Man with Three Eyebrows

One covers his eye to the north
The other his eye to the south
The third one is just below his nose
And just above his mouth

CHORUS . . .
Oh, he's the man with three eyebrows
He dances round and round
He raises the north one to look
The south one to see
The third one to talk and make a sound
He can see what he's talking about
Yes, you can see what he's talking about

6 - Maloney's Bar

Driving along to South Dunedin
Getting there in your own little car
As long as you don't say it's an old bomb
Then you'll get in to Maloney's Bar

Maloney once was an old grey mayor
He ran in the third and he ran in the first
When he was elected then he was neglected
But he's now resurrected to quench your thirst

CHORUS
There'll be a lot of blarney spoken
To get that old authentic feelin'
Many Guinness records will be broken
When wheelin' and dealin' with Whelan

In the old, old days of Dunedin
The Southside was for the working class
In many ways it was an Irish town
With flying ideas, jigs and jugs and glass

Maloney the mayor he came along
And he shouted 'Don't be such a fool'
Drinking and education don't mix
And started up St Patrick's school

CHORUS . . .

We have returned to reclaim the south
We've been away to the world and tried it all
All the book learning and the worm turning
Nothing worked, so we answer the primitive call

To enjoy the Celtic revival
Here we all are, we've come this far
One hundred years have come and gone
And now we're back in Maloney's Bar

CHORUS . . .

7 - O'Ryan and Maher's

Why don't you go out one evening
Look up at the sky and the stars
Just to the side of the Milky Way
You'll see Orion and Mars
      Oh yes, Orion and Mars

Then why don't you come in one evening
To one of the most colourful bars
Order a drink of whiskey and Guinness
From the pub called O'Ryan and Maher's
      Yes, that's right, O'Ryan and Maher's

Well, if you put one and one together
Stargazing and drinking the jars
Your immortal soul will fall through a black hole
And you'll end up on Orion or Mars
      After being at O'Ryan and Maher's

The National Anthem of Occussi-Ambeno

(By the Earl of Seacliff, Poet Laureate)

Recorded in 1983 by the Occussi-Ambeno Revolutionary Massed Choir

In the legends of our dark and dangerous past
When fierce dragons and evil overlords ruled outright
The Seven Ancient Provinces were held in a fast
Tyrannical grip of ignorance and perpetual night
But the inner-soul of the people was ever alight

CHORUS   *The Spirit of the People Shone like the Sun*
                The Spirit of Occussi-Ambeno is Freedom!

The centuries progressed through the tunnel of time
And the long-oppressed People could see a light
The bells of change began to chime
All across the land began the Freedom fight
To weed out the wrongs and set them to right

CHORUS   *The Spirit of the People Shone like the Sun*
                The Spirit of Occussi-Ambeno is Freedom!

From Atanarble in the North, to Quatair in the South
All roads now to Baleksetung in the Centre
From the Eastern Central Range, to the Western River mouth
Extends the Benevolent Rule of our future's creator
Sultan Michael Ismail, our great Leader and Mentor

CHORUS   *The Spirit of the People Shone like the Sun*
                The Spirit of Occussi-Ambeno is Freedom!

Satires

(Satirical pieces from the 1987 novel *Out of It*)

1 - Te Rauparaha's Lament as an Opening Batsman

Kei te anake au
Kei te mokemoke au
Kore rawa hui atu mokemoke
    me kia au puritia koe
Taua kia haere ra muringa he haerenga
    e hoki ki whare kirikiti
Anei taku momoe mongamonga
    i aro i te mana ma kaupapa
Kei ahau he poke
    i roto i taku manawa a wairua
Kei te anake au, no reira
Kei te mokemoke au
Kore rawa hui atu mokemoke
Kei te whakama ahau
    me kia au puritia koe
    e taku taonga porangi, e!
      Aue, aue, awatu ...

2 - Baxter between the Wickets

(a sonnet)

Man! He has called me again
From that place inside me — the unworthy

Servant! He called me three times
When I, in my mortal dung heap mind

Would have settled for one
And all the lice in my beard jumped out

For fear of this terrible century's (looming) speed
Who will torment me now, at night

Who will remind me of Him —
And sin! Which this mad old devil

Commits with every eyelid bat, every thought
Kei te Rangitira o te ngati porangi, ahau —

I stand at the end of the crease, Colin
Knowing He only wants what He knows I can do

3 - Hey man, Wow!

Hey man, Wow! Like the white streak
Of power that provides the purple haze
Which is the universe propelling projectiles
Such as the Red Planet of Mars towards me
The centre of the star-spangled galaxy

There is a theory such as reverse energy
Matter which interpreted into reality
Means, if I flick this switch that's in
My hand in the opposite direction, Mars
Will go flyin', I mean flyin', back

Through the same galaxy of time and space
And over the boundary of infinity
Into eternity — far out, man!
Outside in the distance the wind cries
As the man who is as lost as a child

Throws his round red ball towards
My bat which I hold erect, yeah man!
The wind cries because this blood red ball
Pierces the skin of the air: the wind cries
With the awareness of its own existence

But the ball keeps coming and coming until it hits my
Bat mid-on, and I'm running and the wind is crying . . .

4 - Cricket's Gothic Nature

Ah! How dark
These long-extended wickets and rueful runs
Where nought but bowlers reign, and night, dark
Night
Dark as was chaos 'ere the infant innings
Was rolled together, as black as the pitch
Itself was rolled. The sickly inswinger
By glimmering through the low-browed misty
Defences
Furled round with thy spittle and ropy slime
The ball a supernumerary horror
And serves only to make my night more
Irksome.

5 - Cricket is Strange

Cricket is strange when you're a batsman
Muscles get strained when you're alone
Bowlers seam wicked
The way that they bounce you
Even though they know
Your muscle's been pulled

CHORUS

> *Cricket's strange – runners come out in your place*
> *Cricket's strange – then they fall on their face*
> *Cricket's strange – a funny game*
> *Cricket's strange – all right now . . .*

6 - *from* **The Ballad of Reading Oval**

Yet each man pulls the stumps on himself
By each let this be heard
Some do it with a simple French Cut
And with unflattering word
Cowardly commentators say "Played on!"
Cutting deeper than a sword

Some play careless strokes when they are young
And some when they are old
Some leave such a gap twixt bat and pad
That the ball, like an arrow of gold
Straight to its target blindly goes
Leaving the batsman out in the cold

Some hit too little, some too long
Some wait for an extra or a bye
Some leave the field almost in tears
And some without a sigh
For each man pulls the stumps on himself
Yet none can answer why

7 - **George Gordon's Second Innings**

I want another go! An uncommon want
I didn't like my innings so I'd like a new one
But all cricketing rules and gazettes say I can't
"A second innings in a one-day game is not a true one"

All very well for those with two healthy legs to flaunt
But for those with a foot like mine, it is a ruin –

I think all those bastards who make
Rules for others whilst in their prime
Should be sent to the devil
Somewhat ere their time

8 - Rastaman Declarations (Positive)

I wanna big score
An' it's all right
I wanna hit four
Every day and every night
Shots to the boundary
And a six right over your head

CHORUS
> *Is it four, is it four, is it four*
> *That I'm scoring*
> *Is it four, is it four, is it four*
> *That I'm scoring*

I wanna know, wanna know, wanna know now

Part Four

e tangata, e tangata, e tangata

The Mind of My Lai Revisited

(for David Mitchell)

So this is what happens to our poets
Soft-shoe shuffling along Oriental Parade
The internal massacre about complete
As a handshake equals a kind of recognition

"David," I say, and then repeat my own name
Over and over in an attempt to get through
But your semi-toothless grin and grimace
Tell me you are not here at all

Like a sad combination reminiscent of Groucho
And Harpo without the humour, your spirit
Seems to have deserted you — but I know
Donna Awatere has become yr Remuera Hsfrau —

Achtung, Baby, Babi Yr an' all!

p.s. the ships look beautiful as they glide . . .

Universal Mind

(kia Moana)

i Eclipse

We walked along the path of moonlight
Beyond the artificially lit streets
The waves from the sea washed towards us
On one side, silver-tipped and midnight cool

Into the darker side of the bush-clad landscape
Across the river's bridge, past pumice floating
To black hills highlighted by the lunar sheen
The stars stood clear and individual as they shone

Moving slowly the shadow began to engulf
The moon, whose light flooded the sky
Like the back of a hand over a face
— then she is gone . . .

The familiar night orb left
Only a black orange hole in the sky —
Struggling to understand the no-reason why
Something is missing and resolved . . .

ii Ellipse

Regular oval, traced by a point
And lifting it to your lips
Drink hungrily from the green bottle
The amber liquid that opens the doors of deception

Moving is a plane so that the sum of its distances
Crashes nearer to the earth
Than to the sun, the daddyless son
Will crash, no matter who your father was

From two other points is constant
Male and female (by common concord)
Your left-wing is on fire
From a too greater infusion of brandy jet fuel

And all those right-wing ex-L.S.D. boys in Treasury
So afraid of their own past
That their illusions are complete
The side of the cone makes, Jim! (c.f. HYPERBOLA).

iii (The Third Way)

Regular   Moonlight
        lifting   artificially
              hungrily   washed
                    the one

              Into the
              nearer   past
        The   highlighted
Stars   crash

    From   Shadow
          female   moon
                face   fire
                    she too

              Left those
              only   afraid
        struggling   illusion
makes   something
              There is no fucking third way!

90

While Your Guitar Violently Wails

(to George Harrison)

Despite the high-walls fortress
Of your many-roomed mansion
It seems that living in a convent retreat
Could not keep the madness out

The Beatle-Witch which you
Had become in the mind of a fellow
Liddypoolian was to be extinguished
As an aspect of evil in the material world

Like John, you had become a single fantasy
Of someone's over-rich, heat oppressed mind
Which sought to find the sense of utu
For your success and failure

George, the quiet one, almost eternally silenced
By an eighteen centimetre blade
Beware of sadness and the written word
Which comes back to haunt those who

Scoop it from the cauldron — who sew
The chords of discord in a song

Nuclear Family — A Fragment

In dreams I walked
      Through crowded, confused streets
      Where people, scurrying like rats
            on a sinking ship
      Ran in all directions towards survival

In dreams I moved
      Through a human fog
      It was my single purpose
      That kept me going, and
      Kept me from going insane,
      To find you and the child whom I love

When I saw you in the hall of mirrors
      Like all the other victims
            you radiated decay
      Your hair had shrivelled and gone grey overnight
      I held my arms outstretched
      Hoping you and your child would embrace me
      But you turned away
         and she ran to you, as if I were
               a stranger

I picked up my gun
      And went outside where things weren't quite
            so grim
(I mean this war has killed love
      so what's a pile of rotting bodies)
In my uniform, I watched the beauty of
              another atomic flash
      A tank drove by
        I jumped aboard
        And we headed toward
      The war which can never be won!

For my father in prison, 1965

Doing time
        my father would have needed time to do this
To build a table
        made from matchsticks, our only family heirloom
Matchstick upon
        matchstick held together with some kind of glue
Just like the
        brick building which held him
Yes, that's it
        stone upon black stone which kept him captive
He entered through
        the heavy, bolted steel door they held open
And when he emerged
        he had a matchstick table and was very quiet
Each matchstick
        represented a fragment of his life
Each fragment
        was there outside him, set in glue, and he was a shell

To Cherryl

who in my life is like
the greenstone
precious and hidden
under mountains
and isolated rivers
to the South

like a miner
with a passion
but without a map
I became lost
in my search for you

and as with the stone
it's not your
fault that I
didn't know
where to look

Kia Cherryl

(as translated by Alan Nopera)

ko wai ke i roto i taku ora
he rite ki te Pounamu kahurangi
i ngaro nei i waho i nga maunga
me nga awa o te tonga

e rite au ki te tangata e ki ana
i te kohara
e ngari hore kau he tohutohu
a i taku rapu haere i a koe, ko ngaro au

a ana ki te pounamu
e hara nau te he
kaore au i mohio ana
kei hia koe i ngaro nei

To My Mother

An old photograph
       I look at
(Found it th' other day)

This ol' photograph
       Which I look at
(Long ago is far away)

The old memories
       I think of
(How can my mother be a memory)

This ol' memory
       I think of is you
(And my lovers I also see)

All my lovers are memories
       Deep and dark
(They all remind me of you)

My lovers were they really here
       In the dark
(Or were they always you)

Haiku Trio for
St. Valentine's Day

Litia my love
Within me your life unseen
On snow like a dove

Dark clouds cross my mind
Uncertain of shadows — in
Your eyes strength I find

I sent a red rose
Your children talked and talked and —
Now everyone knows

Watching Ghosts

From hiding places they came to me
An ancient army on the march
Whilst watching Ibsen's 'Ghosts' on TV
The present became the past

My long-dead mother holding her son,
An image in the 'living' room.
A few decades ago her blood had run
When she held me in her womb.

My father was there, a spirit of the air
Who flew in the war and lived
Only to die in a suburb near here,
The blood bursting in his head.

Well, funny old life and all that,
No wonder I feel like little boy lost
While my friends in the room chat,
I sit here watching ghosts.

Revolution Song

my love is sad because . . .
when she looks out at her little garden
all she can see is a fence confining her flowers
bordering her yard, defining her existence

she waits for her children to return from school
and the reggae beat pulses through her dreams
she wishes for trees, for vines, for plants of every colour
her mind becomes a freedom fighter
patrolling her jungle town of the third world
her thoughts move stealthily, carefully they tread
past unexploded bombs and booby traps
wearing jungle-green she moves through memories of
oppression
like a victorious rebel she remembers back
to the time before she grasped liberation
to the time when she knew boundaries and visions of
freedom
and the bully-beatings for stepping beyond U.S.A. or
husband

knowing what she has won by her revolution
knowing she will fight to keep it
my love sits on her afternoon doorstep
with reggae beat pulsing in her ears
and looking out at her little garden
my love is sad because . . .

A minor transition: Platypus to Taniwha — 1974 to 1998

(for Jackie Gilmore)

i

the river time
flows on . . . on comes the new generation
on, the never before seen
on, the never before heard
to become, in time, the never heard of again
as a child after the rain
puts a stick in a roadside gutter
and follows it until it is lost down a drain
so, through the years, the Platypus has seen comings
and goings
observed and taken part
    has been washed away, and has watched
and become Taniwha in the light
    of local truth
But birds still talk to trees
    build nests in their open arms
measure the distance in time, not miles
    in lovers, not lost love
Little wonder that Taniwha has gone to the deep
    And Platypus has lost his identity
All riches is in love
All ruin is in hate
    illustrated thus!
The Platypus sits at the river's edge
    the only light moonlight
    the only light sunlight
and looks into the deep, swift flowing water
    "Haere mai, kia koe
     Haere mai, kia Taniwha e hoa!"
The Taniwha, in the form of a river, stares back
    In incomprehension and flows on!

Now, things are going swimmingly
notwithstanding armed art theft
Hi Jack! As I used to say
We kissed, and I thought of honey, bananas
the salt-sea smell of the open harbour, the wild wind
in our hair — all the surreal memories of paintings, drawings
fish that fly duck-billed through pure, putrid air
and lurid, affluent suburban opulence
where I pulled you across the middle-class
floor of your family's home by your hair
hair so long, so beautiful I that God
had fashioned it!
Every detail I remember, every small movement
and, also, how out of my depth I was . . .

Speculation

(for Melanie)

Walking across old Grafton Bridge to get the bus
I felt a slight nauseous sense of love
A confusion, as when a child long ago
You woke up and didn't know where you were

Earlier in the day I knew I was going to meet
Someone that night, but I didn't count on you
You sitting there thin-faced, slightly wan
I kept my distance for a while

When I finally approached with the usual banalities
You seemed willing enough to talk
Slowly we slipped into the vortex of intimacy
Suddenly here was someone else I knew

As I told stories tinged with hyperbole
You countered with small memories of childhood
While I was out rustling sheep in Otago winters
You, a six year old, secretly saw your father slaughter pigs

Too soon we were lost in the general melee
Social situations mean social courtesies be observed
Although I Felt somewhat at a loss
I acted my part in the general reverie

I soon left the party, however, and caught my bus
Which took me at great speed away from you
As I walked up the last hill towards my home
The night flowers gave off a charming fragrance

Fragile Network

I remember it used to be the fashion
For poets to write about people
Sticking their heads in gas ovens
Or jumping off good old Grafton Bridge

Poets would look upon such people
As heroes or refugees or martyrs
Taking a last stand against the juggernaut
Of modern materialist society

I checked myself early on this point
Considered such subjects self-indulgent
I wanted people to laugh and smile
At what I wrote and did

But now here it is, my poem
To Alan from the south, someone I didn't know
Who stuck his head in a gas oven
Because he couldn't handle something anymore

More, this is a poem to Tahana
(one of many I've written to her)
Who was so sad and broken about Alan's death
She got doped up, out of it, and arrested

And because she tells me of her pain
I must carry it now too
Because I love her —
Yes, it seems I am my sister's keeper

So the fragile network of love and pain
Entwines itself through each other's lives
Like junctions in a silken spider's web
We are all connected, we are all connected

Witches New Year

A starlike light
Seen above Purakanui
Obviously not man made
Unseen observer
Of our dream
Who came to me
And came to me
And came to me
Who carried me
As I carried her
Bare-breasted and quivering
Through ill-lit suburban streets

Flip Side of the Ballad of John and Yoko

6pm News, Tuesday, Ninth of December, 1980
"We have just heard from New York
Ex-Beatle John Lennon was shot today . . . !!!!!!"

i

There I was sitting on a sofa
In one of the southernmost cities of the world
Listening to the radio whilst thinking about cooking tea

Well, how can you be honest about how you feel?

I'd just turned the station over
To get the "real" news of the world
When I heard the words written above: well fuck me!

What else can you do but swear at a time like this

I am thinking about my mother, his mother
Two of the responsible for bringing us into the world
And now John, you're gone! There's only me

Yoko and me, and the rest of humanity together in grief and love

Yoko's in a black scumbag, I left the sofa
Wandered aimlessly around the room the day you left the world
Your death is a climax of events forcing mortality on me

Everybody's talkin' 'bout Pol Pot, Nazism, Socialism, I.R.A. and junkies

Give me a chance, brother
You have helped me understand this world
Now you're dead, am I enslaved or freeeeeeeeeeeeeee!!!!!!!!!

Fuck the revolution, we have bred another generation

ii

When it all began, I was just another
Beatle fan. A teenager from the other side of the world
Looking for something more interesting than school's authority

Distances travelled in space, time and sorrow add up to one thing

Your songs and books helped me discover
In myself, what all the education in the world
Could not; that I could write and illustrate my own story

Knowledge to one is ignorance to another, unless there is love

1968, Hey Jude, the death of my father and mother
Like a lost black sheep I entered the outside world
Sold my records, went to work in a dark, thankless factory

If a person makes enough of one thing, he or she becomes a thing

While I got lost in nothing, you found your lover
For whom you left the Beatles, left the wife, shocked the world
Yoko, through the years of illusion, offered you reality

Eternity may be a stone in Wales, but it is now we must live

And so, lest the press smother
You and your love both withdrew from the world
Which had built you a boat of fame, then left you all at sea

How many oak trees have been allowed to grow from the acorns?

"Just like starting over"
Is not starting over, you are now dead to the world
Sean and Yoko no longer have the shade and strength of their tree

That fallen tree made them a house which they must make a home

iii

We were always a decade away from each other
Yet we were of the same generation
You were the spiritual pathfinder
I followed to the point of penetration
And I never lost you, but let you go

It was not lack of love, but life itself, caused the separation

Now you too have joined the dead and living dead
Who haunt and torment my existence
On this quaint and sadly crazy planet on which
To live is not just to breath, but an insistence
That each such breath is a test of courage and will

Which we understand at a metaphorical distance

Christ!
I know
It ain't easy!

Breaking Beyond

Limited by what we don't know
The conversations breaking beyond
    just out of earshot

The books we have not read
Pages of words breaking open beyond
    in how many other languages?

Other animals understand each other
A wing-flick or hoof breaking ground beyond
    as they move together in their millions

The secret sound of a soul
Whose quietly breaking petals resound beyond
    across the universal divide

Limited by what we know
Like shoreline waves breaking beyond
    our mark is made in shifting sands

Poem to Your Grandmother

i

 digging up the ground
so that her life-long partner
could rest with her
      they found
her long, long silver hair
       pride of her womanhood
had tangled round and round
the root of a breadfruit
          tree
in time, without a sound
woman and tree had merged
she had become nature
out of sight, underground

ii

but, as though to stake his claim
and make her not forget him — not
for something so simple as a breadfruit
             tree
her human lover — I'll say husband
had died
      could only live one year without her, rather
and her breadfruit tree had to give her up

iii

a tree grows on a mound
of earth, under which he and she lie
in death as they had done in life
together now without a sound
woman and man and tree have merged
have become nature and hair and root and heart
out of sight, underground

Bob Dylan, a visitation

(10/9/1998, Wellington)

With my ear to the future
And my mind to the past
Sitting twenty rows back
        and up high
I could feel the real visions of Johanna

From the ancient times
When the nuns had us sing
The answer is blowing in the wind
        the Jews and the Catholics
Have fought pitched battles over my soul

And out on Highway Sixty One
Or along any lonesome railway track
The songs remain like freight cars
        to be sung or shunted
Along the weary lines of a human face

Echoes of Mr. Yeats' hymn
And a thousand singsong others
Expressing in thought, word, music
        like your friend, Woody
The all too familiar taste of dust and death

Recalling the desolate row
Of houses in Margaret Street
Now either destroyed or gentrified
        must we really move
Into the Ponsonby of the new, shallow mind

Later, you entered the 'her'
Part of my life also
With a precious angel
        now gone, but then
I was the man in the long black coat

From all you need is love minus zero
To being sick of love
Then, on one more night
        you took us from Maggie's farm
To forever young, as a simple reminder

Now there's even talk of
Cranking up the Oldsmobile
For so long stuck inside, and
        up the central plateaux
To Auckland, the Great Arsehole, sacred

Okay, Mister Room Man
Play a song for us
Say a prayer too, as you
        wing your own way
Earthbound, heavenwards soaring beyond

For always talking the blues
To your Jews and Gypsies
All those masters of war
        old Hitler, Stalin, and yes
The President of the U.S. does sometimes stand naked

Through all the years' confusions
Of ideas and people and events
To this present listening
        so many things have happened
While you just keep on singing to my sister's alarm

I'm glad to come and see you
To tip my hat to the master's hand
With my rainy day woman
        asleep on my shoulder
Times have changed so much, they've remained the same

I am a stone

I am a poet
I am a stone
The hard rock I am made of
Does not permit growth
The rain falls on me
The wind scours my surface
But I am resolute
Words fly from my weather-worn exterior
Write about it — I can write about it
I am a poet
I am a stone
People come to study what I am made of
And in the past, and in the present
Their conclusions are the same
I remember dancing and . . .
I remember singing
But I can never remember moving
After all, life is movement
Even bacteria moves
      and I can't remember moving
I am a stone

Noa/Nothing I

(an irony)

Rightfully, these words should not be making their way
across the page
Because I am nobody. I have no name and I have no whanau
I am a fragment, the lost piece of a jigsaw
Without mana, without kaha
Without children to continue me, I only live
Kei te noa, ahau — nothing I
Every word I speak scatters to the wind
And is heard only as a sound with no meaning
I have no taste, no smell, no movement
Unseen, I am not even like the invisibility of salt
In a pot of cooking potatoes
Only the darkness knows who I am and silently laughs
Hine-nui-te-po sits waiting
Haurangi, porangi — any Rangi!
Shattered visions permeate my days
When the Rangi of me cries
And the seeds grow within Papa
That's the only connection
And a sadness comes from the only belonging
I am of Te Rangi
And I cannot see or hear the sound of the sea
I am of Te Hau
And I cannot move
I am of Te Ao
And I cannot touch a thing

And what

(to the S9 track gang)

It was familiar
There we were replacing sleepers
Re-laying rails
Tightening bolts with a T-spanner

We trundled back through the cutting
On a jigger
As we heard the down-train
Less than a mile off

As she passed our hut
We talked and smoked
I watched a hawk emulate a wisp of cloud
As they crossed the blue sky separately

These southern coastal hills
Through which our railway runs
Are where I feel at home — here
And the northern city I came from

"Anybody check if there's an up-train in the loop?"
Cried Pascal as our jigger and tray
Loaded with men and spades and shovels
Pulled away up the line

"Oh fuck!" I cried, as I heard
The mournful, relentless
Diesel engine come louder and louder
As it rounded the cutting corner

I ran towards the thing waving wildly
Slipped and fell on ballast and sleepers
I could hear my screams as the iron wheels
Of the steadily slowing engine

And the rails on which it ran
Cut my life in two

Elegy to Lester Bell

(d. 9/9/99)

"Kia ora, Kiwi," the catch-cry
Of a great New Zealand man
Stoic and self-contained
Outwardly gregarious

Yet underneath that all-male
Exterior lay a vulnerability
Which if tapped, would have
Sent the whole pack tumbling

But he had to remain intact
Bringing up three children alone
After the early death of their mother
His beautiful, much loved wife

Working in the tough forestry camps
By day and being a mum at night
Something had to give way
The toughness had to be the winner

When I first met him he was
Enthroned in his huge cane chair
At Taupo where I had gone
With my friend, his daughter, Sandra

And I marvelled at the strength
Of this man whose semi-mocking command
"Sandra!" brought this strong woman
To a simultaneous rebellion and submission

So Lester Bell, the great tree, has fallen
He who wrought the felling of many trees
I watched the life drain slowly away from this proud
Strong man and I kissed him farewell in his final
Stage of vulnerability and release of consciousness
— probably the only time another man could have kissed him

Haere ra, kiwi, Lester Bell
You will be missed, —
The Melling train will miss you
The morning Dominion will miss you
The Rugby Club will miss you
Your workmates will miss you
Your friends and lovers will miss you
Your two daughters and your son will miss you
— and I will miss you —

Haere ra, e Rangatira o te Whare Tane
Haere ! haere! haere!

Skull

(to Tom Scully)

Scully's gone, what will we do?
He drowned in the 'waters of life'
Ushe Baugh, an ancient Irish cure
To be sure, for some, but for others
A delicious, deadly seduction to despair

Scully's gone, what could we do?
He was always the weakest chain
In the link which holds us together
Many times we felt him going,
And now he's gone, left us forever

Scully's gone, what can we think?
The stakes are raised again
The world has turned another notch
Tightening around our precious lives —
The unspeakable has trapped its fox

Scully's gone, what can we feel?
But the sadness and the pain
For the life untimely wrenched
From us, the spiritual amputees,
Our comrade never returned from his trench

Skully's dead, no more to be said
But I'll say it anyway.
I, we, loved you Tom, we feel bereft
The world won't be the same, now
And nor will the life you left

He waiata ki taku tuahine

(a poem to Clare)

Only you could have your fortieth birthday
On a Friday the thirteenth
That Witches' date which spells danger
And excitement in the same breath

But not just any Friday the thirteenth
Either, the last one of the millennium
Like everything in your life a sense of drama
And portent has to be involved —

From the time when you were a baby
When we did our growing up together
Yet apart, you being so much younger
You always had a quality of magic

A quality which said anything can happen
Around here, watch out! And it did —
After our parents died we were separated
And, for a time, lost to each other

Lost to the world, even to ourselves
As we struggled with demons imagined
And real. From the bland nightmares
Of suburban indifference our course was set

Both by accident and design
We were thrown together again and again
Our self knowledge and awareness has come
From acceptance of each other for what we are

So, I salute you, taku tuahine tau
He wahine toa — kia kaha, kia toa, kia manuwanui
Kia ora to you in your struggle for life
A struggle we sometimes share together

Aotea Square —
Centre of Culture

on a Saturday night
with a bottle of stolen wine
I sit in the Square slugging
with a son of Liku
and a son of Glasgow
as we drink and talk and stomp
the elements respond in a fit
of fiery empathy
lightning and thunder
flash and cross across
the barriers of sight and sound
I feel a mimi coming on
as the first thick drops of rain fall
I walk towards the new centre
when I hear the word culture
I reach for my ure
and me and Rangi are crying
tears of joy and defiance
against this monolith
of opulence whose only
function is, as I see it
to partially hide from
view the central police station
and for a few moments
I wish the Aotea Centre
was several stories higher

Part Five

Nga Taiwhanga

a

Nga Haerenga

Walking Beside Shadows in Soft Rain

Walking beside shadows in soft rain
I see faint images of what has been
These shadows form mirages on a wall
Which I see is my life and it is all
Behind me now. All that I have been
Is beyond me like a distant train
And as the train moves further from this station
I look on, filled with anticipation

Onehunga

Onehunga, more factories now in this suburb
Than I can or care to remember

It was one of those places
Where I used to sit in the back of our van

Playing 'eye-spy' with my sisters and brother
While our father drank himself into companionship

Every half-hour or so he would emerge from the pub
Saying, "I've just met so-and-so, I'll only be a minute"

Onehunga, bypassed by time and a new expressway

Oscar Wilde Park

We come here at three o'clock, when saviours die
A portentous time of day, neither
With the light full of midday sun
Nor the blackness of night either
But it seems fitting to celebrate the plaque
At the juncture between light and dark

For it is at such a point
Where Oscar lived his wild life
At once the proud father to a son
And constant husband to a loving wife
Then a darker, more dangerous side embarks
On "a love which dares not speak its name," but hark

The truth lies somewhere in between
The degenerate and uplifting aspect
Of this great and fallen man's compassion
And his very neglect gains our respect
For showing us the two poles of light and dark
For his killing of what he loved we use this plaque
To commemorate his humanity, who heard the lark
Sing, when others only saw mud — I give you
Oscar Wilde Park

Okahu Bay

Dark night, wind off the harbour
Once you approach the sand
The pohutukawa trees surround you
The moon, cut in half and half-hidden by clouds
Provides the only natural light
Each wave that laps at your feet
Has reached you from eternity
The darkness of self, of unremembered soul
The night within embraces my vision
The sadness of each memory
Is like each wave of water
Together they make a flood of tears
Which drown the cries of the heart
This evening you were the moon to me
The only pure light in a life of shadows
Like the moon you too hid behind a veil
Showing light enough for life, but not for love
After a time we left for Okahu Bay
Broke through the line of pohutukawa
I let you walk ahead so you would not see me
Kneel, then kiss the ground,
The ground of my childhood, the ground of my life

Okahu

(as translated by Jean Wikiriwhi)

Kua pouri, ka pupuhi te hau
Mai i te moana,
Hurihuri nga pohutukawa,
Te Marama hangere, kua ahua ngaro i te kapua
Ko tenei anake te maramatanga,
Ke ata papakihia mai e nga ngaru a wae
Ka te pouri au, kua wareware te ngakau,
Ko te po kei te awhi i taku kitenga,
Te aroha ki tena ki tena,
Pera ki ia ngaru o te wai,
Hui katoa, ka heke te manawa,
I tenei ahiahi ko koe
Te marama ki ahau
Ko kou te maramatanga, i tenei ao pouri,
Pera i te marama kahuna kou i
Ko te maramatanga hei oranga, kaore mo te aroha
A, ka wehe mai i Okahu
Ka mahue nga pohutukawa,
Ko koe i mua, kia kore koe e kite i ahau
Ka tuturi, ka kihi i te one,
Ko te one o taku tamarikitanga,
           to one o taku oranga ...

Return Journey

Saturday evening, rain falling down
Waiting for the train
Black hat and dark night
Like taking flight
On some long ago lost express

The darkness without, and the movement
So matched by doubt
We chatter clickety clack
All down the track
Gay in an old fashioned way

Changing trains, up into windy suburbs
The travel itself enough
Happy and light-headed
The thing most dreaded
Happened! The signals were switched

Wake up to techno-funk hangover
A washed out punk
Where's the fire water provider
The great divider
Of black and white world bleakness

As though in reverse, it is day
Never felt worse
In body and spirit
But this time it
Is light and beautiful outside

And the return train makes its way
Along the curve again
Of a beautiful postcard bay
Inside the dark and grey
Inner vision mocks and torments the day

Otara — have a Banana

coming back from the Papatoetoe pub
towards Otara in a Japanese car made for two
I am lolling like a sea-lion in the back

the little car turns the corner too quickly and as
I put my hand out instinctively to stop the roll, it moves into
outer-space as the window shatters on the road

laughing from shock as we cross the motorway overbridge
I see the clouds and sky more clearly with no window
and the fresh breeze quickens my slight hysteria

we pull into the large asphalt covered carpark
which on weekends transforms into a busy market place
but now is only populated by tin ghosts on wheels

leaving my friends I head towards the town-centre
where people shop and smile and talk, listen to music
and the aiitu of you is around every corner

sitting in a cafe I order coffee and a roll
in a gravel-syrup voice, thinking Tom Waitts for no-one
as another mother joins the endless Post Office queue

Reflections on the effect of the 1981 Springbok Rugby Tour on the mentality of the Kiwi

After work the other night
I was feeling all right
It was pay day so I went down for a drink

To a pub I know right well
And I know the clientele
I thought "I'll be welcome here tonight I think"

When I first walked in the door
My mate said "Have one more"
Even before a drink had passed my lips.

Another fellow, already frisky
Said, "I'll get you a whiskey"
And came back with a brandy and some chips.

And so before too long
Conversation and song
Mixed together, with alcohol to lubricate the voice

Have a gin, and have a rum,
Have a beer, a wine, come, come,
It's my turn now boys what's your choice?

Soon I was better at talkin'
Than I'd ever been at walkin'
My legs were like my mind, that is not straight.

By now my head was swimmin'
And I was looking at all the women
Thinking, that one, no that one, no that one would be great.

I went out for a wee wee
And I thought, I'm at the Kiwi
No wonder everything here is so friendly and bright.

And I thought about the past
How often I'd spent my last
Penny here, long ago, every single night.

For when I was a student,
Earnest, right and prudent,
It was coming to this pub that turned me on my head

For I could have been a teacher,
Doctor, lawyer, even a preacher,
But I went to the Kiwi, so I'm a drunken poet and labourer instead

Memories are sad, enough of this!
I thought and finished off my piss.
Having done what's done I must do what I must do.

As I stumbled to the bar
Which seemed five times as far
I bumped into ten or twenty boys in blue.

I thought, I've seen them before
Was it Gisborne, Hamilton or
No, it was just down the road at Eden Park.

And it's not that long ago
Or is my memory just slow
To forget that cloud that hung over our country long and dark?

Well I tried to have a talk,
And I watched the blues baulk
When they said "The manager has asked you to leave."

The ones who wielded batons
Are the same ones that we spat on
Aotearoa is such an easy place to grieve.

I think I shall not deign
To enter this hotel again
I was so drunk I didn't want to cause a fuss

When I got outside it cleared my head
I forgot all that had been said
My main preoccupation was to catch a bus

Bastion Point — Koha 22/5/88

Watching Koha last night
While people talked of pots and pans rattled
— it was like trying to understand
surrealism when all you feel is anger
The bland, semi-digested meal of television
feels heavy in the gut
— some things just won't break down

As those army trucks
Rolled along the waterfront drive towards Orakei
The politics of Muldoonery (inherited from
the orange North of Ireland) was revealed
Five hundred police surrounded
Old men and women, children and dogs
Young female and male warriors

All received the great Kiwi Koha
as the flightless bird blundered around
The ordinary bloke had struck a blow
For democracy — As with Rua, as with 1951
as with 1981 — this hapless nocturnal stuck
its beak out. When the first Great New Zealand
1kg explodes we'll know the worm has turned

South Sea Doggerel

Who gives two figs
For the death of two pigs
Clubbed to death by old Paul Reeves

When they've been cooked
They taste as good as they looked
When wrapped up in coconut leaves

Rather, save your regrets
And your liberal frets
If you must make a song and a dance

For the murderous attacks
On nineteen Kanacks
Fighting to shake the shackles of France

from : Fantastic Modern Japanese Travelling Alphabetical Haiku

A queue, waits in line
The train pulls in the station
Leaves again at nine

B.Q. Bar B.Q.
We had fried steak and eggs, then
Got back home by 2

C.Q., I seek you
My love, I need your soft touch
To build me anew

"Dee queue is too long
I'm a leavin town" says the
Negro in Hong Kong

Equal no more, bound
The two friends struggled to find
Their lost common ground

"Far queue! Far queue!" cried
The porter directing the crowd
"Near queue! Sorry, I lied"

"Gee, there's a cutie!"
Ejaculated old Jones.
Mrs. Jones drank tea.

H.Q. sent a note
"Japanese Haiku used for
Secret codes; no joke!"

IQ was too high;
Libido too low, Hari
Kari was answer. Why?

My cue, to come in
Was "She'll open the door at
Midnight." I went in

O, quiet the night
Snow fell, an owl flew nearby
In the pale moonlight

Rescued from the sea
The fishermen all replied
"I'd love a whiskey!"

Xyster is sharp now
Bones are cleaned, turned into flutes
Let's make music, now

Zephyr, West wind to
You a poem was written
This is mine, Mark II

Dunedin Paraclete

Up the old Mt. Cargill road
With the darkness of night
Enshrouding my car like a fog

I can only see as far ahead
As my headlights penetrate —
Out of the blackness comes

From the left-hand corner
Of my windscreen, like an omen,
An albino owl which fans

Its pure white wings wide
Open as far as they will
As it lands on the roadway

Forcing my vehicle to stop
In its ready made tracks
And for several minutes

The nightbird stands caught
Deliberately in the main beam
Like a centre stage actor

Then, having spoken its silent
Unspoken soliloquy, the bird
Takes flight from my perception

I am left to continue my
Journey, emboldened by this
Visitation from the future

Three Paekakariki Fragments

as dusk darkened
               the surrounding hills
looked like they were
               folding towards the beach
the sky, thick-clouded,
               mirrored the choppy
waves which quietly rolled
               onto the black sand
and something alien
               caught my vision
a large, black, pointed fin
               beyond the white breakers
but near enough to
               the shore to hear me
talking to it. Later,
               I told people that
I took my pet shark
               for a walk tonight . . .

-

a large piece of driftwood, whose eyes followed us, pale,
as we walked along the night-falling sand,
was a seal so tired after surviving, and
being chased through the deep, deep sea by a killer whale

-

moonlight shimmered brightly, dancing lightly
          on the nightdark water
outside the cliff-descending train window
          between
Muri and the taonga-filled memories of the
historic, present-day Paekakariki Station
the railway could be travelling through any
exotic, romantic, love-enhanced landscape
          in the world . . . and it is!

Que Pasa New York, Statue of Liberty Said Come!

The Whollyweird images
Of the burning, violated twin peaks
Towering infernally over our TV dinners
Nightly

The Big Apple
As vulnerable as any
Other organic creature, agonised
Quietly

Because the sound was down
And people you know, only
Live a couple of blocks away
Lightly

The death of innocents
And of innocence itself
No matter how wrongly or
Rightly

The U.S.A.'s sins
Visited upon its biggest
Brightest symbol-city
Unsightly

And unseemly revenge
The bald eagle has come home
To roast, no longer
Flightly

But retarded and
De-feathered, even the president
Despite his threats of war, looked
Slightly
        fazed, dazed, uncertain . . .

Down through the Lampgrain

(catch a falling star)

the dusk deepens

and the darkly-lit night

creeps towards our destination

as we travellers are revelling

— back out of the long tunnel

from the city

and along the local track

through back yard lupins

passing unter den Linden

down through the Lampgrain

to Porirua

we all, as one, recognise

some greater destiny

It's not the Leaving of Wellington

(for Moana)

i

The ferry backs from the downtown dock
Turning its prow to the harbour's head
Seeing the city with a Lilliputian eye
With its toy train set and slot car motorway
Connecting the shoreline from bay to bay

Talk of leaving is all in the past for me
Now that I live out my diminutive life
Amidst these hills and long, low valleys
Each joined by wires and strips of tar
And iron rails all binding us from afar

With the intimate knowledge of many lovers
Each suburb, each area reveals mysterious charms
Small delights oft unseen or passed by
Unless perceived from that special point of view
Which sees in familiar scenes, life anew

Or, even if the talk is of one love only
Throughout the many years of daily existence
Who, with witty surprise recreates the mundane
Everyday hours, spicing them with endless changes
Within the well-worn path of constant rearranges

Wellington is the one of whom I speak
The many-headed fish of an ancient tale
From Whanganui-a-Tara and the inlets to
Te Ngati Poneke, up and down Hutt's corridor
Out to Porirua, Te Rauparaha's Kapiti shore

Many are the moods of sky and harbour
Brooding Aztec hills of dark and gold combine
With lightness of slow meandering streams
Turning suddenly to racing torrents overnight
Whose beauty beholds again to set things right

So, rather than leaving old Wellington town
I search for reasons to stay, not to go
Exploring with intimacy to understand
This alien city and landscape, without reservation
Formerly Nicholson's Port and a Railway Station

ii

By a church we sat, by a wayside road
The dark-brick building reflected the sky
And time of day, almost dusk, the colours
Dark-bright green, the red almost blood
Contrasting hues emphasising our mood

From this nineteenth century ancient scene
Our union was forged and as we walked
Through Johnsonville Mall towards the train
Our love was tinged with shadowed light
As the world is divided into day and night

Once aboard the train back to Wellington
Even the carriages evoked an earlier time
This line was once on the main trunk
Is now a branch, almost a twig in size
A once proud railway almost in disguise

However, even the narrowest gauge is prone
To Romance and thoughts of faraway places
Station names give rise to fantasies, thus
Simla Crescent becomes the fine and large
Refuge for the bureaucrats of Wellington's Raj

As the miniature train set of this line
Descends down through the Ngaio Gorge
The darkness into which the world plunges
Of tunnels, emerging only intermittently
To countenance many a road-lined tree

Then bursting out of the bushes
Like the famed chariot of Cortez
To behold in our sight an Inca city
Half golden and half black decay
A jewel set in a sombre, sparkling bay

iii

At Lambton Interchange, where train
And bus, and car merge and become one
Where overhead wire, underwheel rail
Together with the tarseal of the road maker
Intertwine to disperse the earth quaker

The fear which all people live with
In this capital city is the ground opening
Like a sacrifice to the hungry beast
Of beehive drones and Cathedral bricks
All swallowed by the monster's tricks

The stadium to serve as afters, and
The downtown centre of commerce
From old financial Featherston Street
To the lights and shops of Lambton Quay
Would all be swept to harbour and to sea

iv

Te taniwha of historical Tinakori Road
Winds its way from Thorndon towards
Kelburn, where Cable Car meets the park
And harbour views that define the university
Through the bush pops-up the mushroom city

Echoes of the last tram to Northland
Are heard in the still extant tunnel
As heading further on to Karori
Travelling through a no-man's-land
Where glade and wooded areas stand

Past the municipal cemetery buildings
With grave and headstone echoing the dead
Leading like an allegory into antique
Shoppes, recalling glories of the past
Where the old is first and first is last

Beyond the centre of suburban gehenna
An anniversary at a Thai Restaurant
Then winds the road up, then downwards
Gone are the binding rails and wires
Replaced by metaphorical funeral pyres

Parking the car under a tree's cool shade
Washing our hands at the shed-side tap
In deference to the tapu on the place
You go and visit your departed friend
While I talk to a magpie at the other end

Leaving Makara, climbing the steep incline
Looking back with a hawk's-eye view
Of the bright blue sea through green trees
After not long we are back amongst the wall
Of city-side concrete and glass edifices so tall

v

Making a visitation to the Blessed Virgin
At St. Mary's of the Angels, we pray
The beauty and tranquillity of the church
With intimate stained glass and figurines
Gives us respite from Yellban and city machines

Diving down into the midtown area of retail
Therapy, two dollar shops, more and more
Manners Mall where jugglers, clowns and vagrants
Hang out, waiting for the main or smaller chance
While others go to movies, dig music, busk or dance

I, laughing, say "take me to Cuba Mall"
A pretend hijack pistol in my hand
An infidel mocking the people's revolution
Happily, we head to second-hand bookshops
Past a mixed-bag of coffee bars and bus stops

vi

The trolley-bus ascends the curved hill
Past Aro Street, the once bohemian centre
Reaching Brooklyn, whose Big Apple image
Rotates like the latter day windmill
Solitary sitting, a sign atop a bleak hill

The trolley tootles off to Funky Kingston
Telling of the Magic Bus to Happy Valley
Passing rubbish dumps and gorse bushes
Where such a 'trip' will end no-one can say
But a psychedelic finger points to Owhiro Bay

Then we move crab-like along the drive
Which passes all the outer rim of bays
Island, Lyall, Breaker and many others
Ending up at Seatoun, the seaside town
Whose stormy reef brought the Wahine down

Seatoun also has another visage
More pleasant and secure than stormy seas
It is where the whanau live, so I go
Often alone to visit, before heading back towards
The city by bus, along well defined corridors

Passing the crazy airport runway
Where shoot out over the road
And heading more and more into suburbia
Missing closely beyond the famous Miramar
The infamous Mt Crawford Prison, seen from afar

Kilbirnie Cats are fighting but remain unheeded
As our vehicle follows its overhead trajectory
Down, down, down into old Newtown
Where multi-cultural stores and people
Punctuate with music, colour and church steeple

vii

Getting off at the Taranaki Street stop
I head to the revamped Courtenay Place
In this up-town area we meet again
Not far from the first fateful night
Of our time together, when I took flight

From the arms of Molly Malone's
Into yours, I had been on the whiskey
And stout and they threw me out
Now we walk that ancient treaded path
Of our aroha, in its future and its aftermath

As our waka now breaks the shadow
Of Mount Vic and moves through new
Elongated dark shades from the upbeat
Stalinesque architecture of Te Papa
We rest take a frugal repast for our supper

viii

Along the spaghetti highway or pasta
Main vibrato rail to the Hutt Valley
We travel, reaching the rundown grandeur
Of Petone Railway Station which branches out
To Melling, or on to the main suburban route

Where the Ava gardener tends his plot
And skinhead graffiti offers threats
Black thoughts caught in crazy bald heads
Then the train turns sharply to the left to
Cross the river and meet its Waterloo

Past Pomare, son of another waiata aroha
To count the cars on the Silverstream
Turnpike, we've come to look for another car
In a triumph of British engineering skill
The Irish Rover takes us over Haywards Hill

Down into the Porirua Basin we drive
Then, pushing the supermarket trolley, we
Count down the days and many hours
When we will live in our Hacienda by the sea
Our Spanish daze shimmering in Paekakariki

Where we live and love and play with shells
And land and sea creatures of many hues
Where we swim, and you take Dogwog walking
And, driving up the Paraparaumu mini-golf range
Or, on the evening verandah watching sunsets change

Things move on, we no longer live under
The same roof, yet our lives still intertwine
Along a line of towns from Tawa to the crossing
Of McKays. It's not the leaving of Wellington
But the love lines which connect us on and on

ix

Some things from the past can only be illusion
And people and places only alluded to
As a duck wades down to a Lindale pond
Where Whitireia builds the old anew
So, forgotten suburbs are rejuvenated too

'Nai Nai' reads the destination on an old bus
Waiting in a shed for rest and restoration
The things which bind the past to the present
Are now shared, as a misled missing generation
Struggles to make its relevance to the nation

All the dreams and wishes that can be borne
By the progress of a water-borne diseased insect
Have oft clogged the means of communication
Leaving us all without hope or respect
Whose failure is through ignorance not neglect

Wellington lies caught between two worlds
Almost an island isolated, but at the end
Of another island, a fish head left to rot
Swelled by self-importance, playing pretend
To the rest of the country's off end

But within each soul is a separate story
And inside each place is a unique tale
So, we have explored in microscopic vision
A city in general guise, and in close detail
Two lives and their love within that pale

For cities are nothing without their people
E tangata, e tangata, e tangata, hear the cry
Of song and love, of tears and laughter
Attempting to answer the ancient question: why?
It is for all our worths that we must try

Wellington of Ngati Poneke, and its skyline
Defined by its high hills and low lying
Valleys, like a reflection of the inner soul
Whose struggles with light and darkness bring
Extremes of the human heart between which we swing

Songs of a Tokio Greengrocer

i

Tokio Central
A bullet train fires, mushroom
Crowd, Hiroshadow

ii

Alles verfallen
Axis old as love, pasta
Melon, cauli, fish

iii

Ginza, people walk
Everywhere, street lanterns ignite
My vegetables

iv

Don't assume Basho
Azuma Bashi Poets
Free delivery

v

Seed of Edo grow
After Kyoto reclaim
Tall trees scrape skywards

vi

Orders tomatoes
But streets have no names, so Yu
Tu gets potatoes

vii

Ticket gets you there
Chikatetsu — walkway
Or apples and pears

viii

Amidst Aoyama
And Ikebukuro lies
The real city, small

ix

Diet library
Rice paper, turn lettuce leaves
Look, Sushi cook book!

x

Hana Kawado
And her sisters, Senso Ji,
Asakusa peach

xi

Nartia welcome!
From Hameda visit friends
Take a fresh cabbage

Thursday Night at the Naval and Family

Listening, looking, thinking and remembering

First, listening to the island band
     same old songs week after week
     the rhythm moves my feet
     and the drink and smiles
     make me feel like I'm sort of at home
     the voices and the words
     foreign and familiar

Looking out the window at O'Malley's Corner
     and following with my eyes
     past other Karangahape Road neons
     up to the lines of old Auckland roof-tops and sunset sky
     then inside seeing
     all the pretty girls dancing
     talking and singing and smoking cigarettes

Thinking why am I here and
     why do I keep coming to this place
     where some nights I'm the only local
     although I can't see that
     and no-one else seems to notice
     and the foreigner I've been all my life
     doesn't exist here

And remembering the Pacific Island music
     my mother used to play on the gramaphone
     and the Pacific Island woman
     who shared my life
     and dreams for a short while
     as the music wafts over me like waves
     I stare into my glass with anger at separation

Moving again — overnight train

Moving again
even the moon looks good tonight
full and bright
       first on one side of the train, then the other
My pounamu has returned to me
       amidst fragments of pain
       but everything has its price
Moving again
       feeling hollow and happy
ready for anything that comes my way
       words are beginning to make themselves heard
as they trivialise and enhance reality
       destroy to create
       degenerate into life
       blood alcohol through my veins instead of love
       but it's just the other side
       and the separation is complete
my pounamu has returned
my kaha must come from my heart
and we are rockin' through the night
train wheels rollin' round and round
like the brandy in my brain
one book of poetry costs three cans of beer . . .

Last time I was on this train I was so in love with you baby!!!

The Earl's Progress

So drunk that he could live without love
So drunk he pissed against a car in the main street
He stole, and disobeyed other commandments
He accosted perfectly decent people with his story
He lied to himself about poetic licence

But as he stumbled to the final bar that night
He summoned all his aristocratic nobility
And with neither rhyme nor reason, nor recognition
                nor recollection of anything
The Earl uttered with a religious fervour
                that sublime word, "Cognac!"

A Penrose Pineapple

(for David Eggleton)

industrial grey
backgrounds this
red-blue bordered
painting as though
some punk Gauguin
gotta hold of
the notion that
the Pacific Ocean
needed some
sorta expression
for its time and place
industrio-tropical
and a real
Penrose high is
resultant, subject to
flecked fruit
red — yellow — green
zig-zag jagged
edges behind which
lies Christmas Island
Happy New Year
on Mururoa
and the pineapple
is number one fruit
on the menu at
Atomic Café, Tokyo
branch-line to
Onehunga via Te Papapa
bullet train, bomb train
no time (fragmented)
like the present
shunted reality
nuclear free, unclear future

"Bravo! Bravo!" its
the U.S. Marshall Islands
playing in the Pacific basin
and the Penrose pineapple
says enjoy your
full half-life

Remuera Dreamtime

(for Maria)

It's walking down the road
Where the hedges and the fences
Loom tall, the trees are tall
Beautiful and stilted

The light is the evening
Colours in the unmoving silence
It's the dream and it's the time
Of day and of life

Mercedes and copulating dogs
Are the only people on the street
It doesn't go near them
Because they get angry

And then at night the
Sharp sound of husband
And wife fighting, baying
Like dingoes in the dark

It rained in the morning
And the bus could be heard
Moving and shifting further down
Somebody's disturbed the Rainbow Serpent . . .

from its sleep in the deep waterhole

6.15 Waiheke Ferry to Auckland, Wednesday 20 July, 1983

The line of the low hill undulates
As I keep my head still
And let the boat do all the . . .
                              movement

Darkness shrouds my journey but
There is light
In the sky the stars and the moon shine like pearls
Waves break along the bow
White foam almost frozen by the cold
I am in tune with the natural melancholy
I move like an iceberg from shore to shore

For me this is the end of journey and beginning
Dressed in black, I resign
For years I have travelled in pursuit
You made sure I was always one step behind
Covered your trail whenever I got close

From the safety and calm of the bay
The ferry now sails into open waters

Rangitoto reminds me of you
Looks the same from any angle
Except close-up
But the sky is not on fire tonight
And, if I am alight it is with the fire of ice

Two lovers come on deck
They feel the chill in the night air
When they turn and see me, dark and still
Perhaps they feel another chill . . .
                              they leave for the cabin

This evening takes on a rare quality
This boat could be anywhere
                    if it weren't so cold
We might be travelling from
                    one Greek Isle to another
And I might be anyone
                    instead of thinking of you
I could be in the warm arms of a lover . . .
But I wouldn't have it any other way
Austerity has a beauty all its own

I try to imagine from which position
North Head was named
Why not South Head etc
You are fading from me
I am being engulfed by the lights
                    and distractions of the city
I try to think of why I love you
But things are moving too fast
                    the boat is making up lost time
                    the boat is making up lost time
With Auckland upon us people emerge from inside
I find I am talking to someone
                    he has been chopping trees at his section

My friend who waits for me on the wharf
Greets me with a jovial "Hello sailor!"
Immediately I get ashore we go to a pub
Where I down a double whiskey to break the ice

Self Deception

(a poem from the novel, Unlevel Crossings)

Snow was falling on the small railway station
The ground was as cold as the air
The only heat rose from the engine's boiler
Whose steam billowed out of its funnel
Spilling over on to the platform
Obscuring the already chaotic scene

Our guards were rounding up old women
Children, and lame and crippled men
Herding them into freight wagons
As I crossed the mesh of railway tracks
Towards the Belsen-bound death express
Out of the crowd came a small boy, smiling

The child was dark and Jewish-looking
And one of our men was yelling at him
To hurry up and get into the boxcar
When suddenly the boy turned away
And became light and ethereal looking
He floated off into the approaching evening air

As the vision joined the engine's rising smoke
I realised I was watching myself
All those years ago at this station, waiting
To get the train home from my school
Catching a final glimpse towards the clouds
The evaporating image smiled back down

HeadworX

Series Editor: Mark Pirie

New Poetry

Pocket Fiction